SIGN LANGUAGE

SIGN LANGUAGE

.

.

.

AND OTHER TALES
OF MONTREAL WILDLIFE

JOSH FREED

Véhicule Press

The stories in this book first appeared in the *Montreal Gazette* in one
form or another. Most have been updated, combined or otherwise revised.
Thanks to Ingrid Peritz, my in-house editor, and Victor Dabby,
my out-house editor, as well as Jon Kalina, Gerry Bergeron,
Tom Puchniak, Stephen Phizicky, and Sheila Arnopoulos for their
many ideas. Philip Fine helped prepare and edit the final manuscript.
The publisher wishes to thank Terry Mosher, Tony
Harpes, Don Arioli, and Vicki Marcok for their assistance.

Published with the assistance of The Canada Council.

General editor: Simon Dardick
Cover design: JW Stewart
Cover illustration by AISLIN
Imaging by ECW Type & Art, Oakville, Ontario
Printed by Les Editions Marquis Ltée

CANADIAN CATALOGUING IN PUBLICATION DATA

Freed, Josh, 1949-
Sign language : and other tales of Montreal wildlife

ISBN 1-55065-013-0
1. Montreal (Quebec) – Anecdotes. 2. Quebec (Province) – Anecdotes
I. Title

FC2947.3.F73 1990 971.4′28′00207 C90-090546-8
F1054.5.M84F73 1990

Distributed in Canada by University of Toronto Press,
5201 Dufferin Street, Downsview, Ontario, Canada M3H 5T8
and in the United States by Bookslinger, 502 North Prior Avenue,
St. Paul, Minnesota 55104 and by University of Toronto Press,
340 Nagel Drive, Buffalo, N.Y. 14225-4731.

Véhicule Press, P.O.B. 125, Place du Parc Station, Montreal, Quebec H2W 2M9

Printed in Canada on acid-free paper.

CONTENTS

INTRODUCTION

∙

∙

∙

MONTREAL: **ROOF ON THE LOOSE.** *A strong windstorm yesterday snapped cables and blew away the roof of the $1-billion Olympic Stadium. The airborne roof was last sighted heading south, across Lake Ontario.*
  Space stations are tracking it.

No, it hasn't happened, but when it does — admit it — you probably won't be surprised. You'll say: "Oh well, that's Montreal . . . Weird things are always happening there. Lucky it didn't hit a jumbo jet."

And you'll be right. Strange things *are* always happening in Montreal, the crisis capital of Canada. The Big O and Olympic woe, terrorist bombings and language problems, Meech and Mohawks: even if you don't live in Montreal, you read so much about it you might as well be here.

If Quebec is Canada's distinct society, Montreal is its distinct city, with one foot in French Quebec, the other in English Canada, and both feet tripping over each other. Politically, Montreal is a microcosm of Canada. It is where East meets Ouest and French élan meets English bland: an uneasy household where the two solitudes must sleep together under the same roof.

Our conjugal life affects the whole country. Even if you live in Mississauga or Medicine Hat, you're likely to get pulled into our quarrels. To paraphrase John F. Kennedy: in this country, we are all Montrealers — which isn't as bad as you think. Despite the kerfuffle over separatism and the language war, we get along pretty well on the streets of Montreal, where we rarely quibble over language. We've got too many other things to worry about.

In a nation of tame, law-abiding commuters, our city is a ride on the wild side, an exercise in controlled chaos. Our roads are the Beirut of traffic: a high-speed hell featuring kamikaze couriers, cannonball buses, and wrong-way cylists, with kids dangling from the handlebars like fur dice.

Our potholes resemble tank traps, our construction zone detours are labyrinths from which many drivers never return. Our pedestrians are urban *muhajhadeen*, courting death every time they go out for milk. Put your hand out to stop traffic in this town and you are likely to lose it.

It is survival of the fastest.

There is also our distinct geography. Glance at a map and you'll see that nothing in this city is where it's supposed to be. Montreal East is really in the north end; Westmount — our legendary West-end district — is deep in the east end. As the Michelin guide to Canada points out, Montreal is the only city in North America where the sun rises in the south. Even a homing pigeon would get lost.

Our city poses other difficulties. Our winters are as bleak as Ottawa's night life, our summers bring out man-eating mosquitoes as savage as Newfoundland priests. Our urban wildlife includes black flies, white elephants and Green Onions — an elite parking police so vigilant it will ticket a double-parked wheelchair. For anglophones, there are additional challenges. You must walk softly and carry a big French-English dictionary. You must know two pronounciations for every street: Notre Dame and Noder Daim, Rue St Jacques and St. James.

You must know how to read between the signs.

Living here can be frustrating and infuriating, exotic and exhausting — but it is well worth the effort. I have lived briefly in other Canadian cities. Edmonton was too safe, Toronto got up too early. Vancouver never got up at all. Montreal rarely sleeps, and neither do I, which is part of the reason we get along.

I like eating smoked meat at 2.00 a.m., and celebrating lunchtime with a "festival of steak and beer"; I like the fact that we are so eager for celebrations, even Moving Day becomes a mass holiday. I like turning on the news and never knowing what's going to happen next: a bus strike, an evacuation of the Metro and the Big O. Or a blank TV screen, because "solar flares" have blacked-out power at Hydro-Quebec.

There is something in this chaos that nourishes me, something in the adversity that makes my adrenalin flow. As an aging hooker on "The Main" once told me: "I like to hear the city going Boom, Boom, Boom."

Even when it is the sound of police gunfire.

Most of the stories in this book are about life in Montreal: big city life, neighbourhood life, my life. They're about the crazy things that can happen in any city.

They just seem to happen here more often.

Josh Freed
October 1990, Montreal.

Wildlife and Wheel Life

ALL ROADS LEAD TO IBERVILLE

•

•

•

BIENVENUE À MONTRÉAL say the signs that greet visitors driving into our city. Welcome to Montreal — if you can find it. Chances are you won't, unless you already live here.

Like most residents here, I am a battle-hardened motorist. I decipher obscure pictograms; I decode unilingual road signs like RISQUE DE BROUILLARD and ETEIGNEZ VOS PHARES; I am always poised over the steering wheel like a fighter pilot, ready to swerve across three lanes of traffic for last-second exits that have had no prior warning.

But I often wonder about U.S. tourists. How do they cope with signs that switch to both kilometres and French the moment they cross the border? How do they deal with our beat-up roads, our bullying drivers, our baffling road signs? How do they make their way into Montreal?

I recently had a chance to find out while driving home from Burlington, Vermont. Shortly after crossing back into Quebec, I stopped for a small car on the side of the road, its emergency blinkers flashing. Inside was a slight grandmotherly figure, clutching the steering wheel like a life preserver.

"Thank goodness you stopped," she said, as I pulled alongside. "I'm looking for the way to Mon-ray-all?"

Her name was "Endy." She was a plucky, grey-haired physician from Ogunquit, Maine, driving to Montreal for the first time. She said she had "buzzed through the States in four hours flat," following wide highways and well-marked signs to Montreal. But everything had changed when she crossed into "Kwee-bec."

"Nothing indicates the way to Montreal," she said. "I decided to pull over, before I disappeared into the sunset."

As I looked at this innocent American visitor, it seemed time for a small experiment. I gave her instructions — stay on the same highway and look out for Route 35 — but as she puttered off in her old Chevette, I swung in behind and surreptitiously followed her.

The road from the U.S. border to Montreal is a grim affair: a three-lane highway lined with *frites* stands, firecracker stores, and tacky junkshops displaying a century of debris — from rotting wagon wheels to abandoned tractors.

It is the main route from Vermont to Montreal — but you'd never know it to read the road signs. Every junction indicates the way to a colourful choice of little-known Quebec towns:

ST-VERONNE À PIKE RIVER. IBERVILLE.
ST-VENICE-EN-QUEBEC. IBERVILLE.
HENRYVILLE. CLARENCEVILLE. IBERVILLE.

All roads lead to Iberville (a town of 8,547 people), none to Montreal. In the first half hour of the trip, there were 26 signs for Iberville — only four to Montreal.

Endy seemed more and more confused. After each junction she slowed to a crawl, scouring the roadside for a sign to Montreal — but rarely finding one.

She pulled off the road twice for information, and forty-five minutes into the trip, her luck ran out. A large bridge loomed in the distance, and the road split. Straight ahead was a sign:

SAINT-JEAN.
BOUL. DU SEMINAIRE.

To the right, another sign:

ST-JEAN.
BOUL DU SEMINAIRE SUD.

No mention of Montreal.

Paralysed by the choice, Endy slowed to a near-stop — but the drivers behind her pounded on their horns. She swerved off the exit, heading into the town of St. Jean. I waited at the exit, and eventually, Endy's little car puttered back onto the highway to try again.

A full moon hung like a battered softball in the sky. Dusk was falling, and slowly Quebec's highway landscape unfurled its charms.

A rusted car, impaled on a pole, to advertise a garage.

A 20-foot dummy in a Coke t-shirt, outside CANTINE CHEZ JOJO.

There were signs for LAPINS À VENDRE and DANSEUSES A GO-GO NUES. There were more pictograms of snowmobiles and more junctions — for Richelieu, St. Luc, Laprairie. Then, another huge sign:

FIN 35.
2 KM. JCT 10.

Could Endy speak French? I knew the sign meant the "end" of Highway 35 — but did she? Or would she think it meant: 35 miles to Fin, Quebec.

Two kilometres later: the highway ended.

The road narrowed and Endy ploughed on. In the dark, I spied a small exit on the far right, with a nearly invisible sign for Montreal. There were skid marks all over the highway from last-second turns by other drivers — but Endy never saw the exit. She disappeared down the long dark road, heading toward the town of Sorel, 80 kilometres away.

My experiment was turning sadistic. It was time to help out before the lady vanished. I chased after Endy to flag her down and she greeted me like a long lost friend.

"Thank goodness you spotted me. The highway was so dark, I knew it must be the wrong road — but I had no idea where to find the right one."

She had known that fin meant the end of the highway — but "there was nothing at the 'FIN' to tell me where to go. I was never sure where I was heading, except for someplace called 'Eye-berville.'"

"Are they trying to hide Montreal?"

I said I was a journalist, and offered to lead her into town, but Endy volunteered to go on alone to uncover more traps for the "next victim."

And so we continued the final 35 kilometres, past more snowmobile crossings and more moose crossings, more junctions with signs for Endy to decipher.

BROSS. 3 PROCHAINES SORTIES
BOUL. TASCHERAU. BOUL. MILAN. LAPRAIRIE.

Occasionally, there were signs for Montreal.

Just before the city, Endy saw her first English-language sign, a giant billboard warning: LEFT LANE FOR ONCOMING BUSES. She swung quickly to the right, and missed the sudden left-lane exit for the bridge leading downtown. I chased after her again and steered her back on route, before she ended up in the two-mile long Louis-Hippolyte Lafontaine Tunnel taking her toward Quebec City.

By the time we reached Montreal, Endy looked as if she'd run a marathon. It had taken her two-and-a-half hours to cover 100 kilometres — an average of 40 kilometres an hour.

"It could have been worse," she said. "If I hadn't met you, I'd have been out there all night."

I left her at a friend's house in Westmount — but she was planning to drive to Quebec City the next day and feared more problems. I recommended a map — and asked her to phone when she got back. Several days ago, I found a message on my answering machine. I reproduce it verbatim.

Good morning. This is Endy from Maine, whom you guided into Montreal, in your Cinderella coach. Thank you again.

I'm back from Kweebec City, and I must tell you that I managed to get to my destination safely. I had a wonderful time, including a fine drive there and back.

There was little difficulty with either the signs or the roads . . . but I must add that I profited by experience.

This time, I took the bus!

A DEFENSE OF OUR HIGHWAYS

•

•

•

Why are the roads so bad in Quebec? Some people blame the situation on poor engineering and maintenance, but I have my own theory: Quebec's highways are secretly managed by its Department of National Defense.

China long made map-making illegal to discourage foreign invaders. England reversed its road signs during World War II, to stymie a German invasion. Quebec obviously has a similar strategy.

With no provincial army and a long unprotected border with the U.S. our roads are the only major obstacle protecting us from invasion. Imagine what would happen if American tanks ever tried to cross the border. Their generals would soon be hunched over French dictionaries, baffled by SENS UNIQUE signs and pictograms of snowmobiles; bewildered by the absence of road signs for Montreal.

Half the troops would get lost in Iberville. The rest would never get past the end of Highway 35. I can hear the commander shouting into his walkie-talkie:

"*That* little exit for Montreal? Don't be ridiculous! — it looks like it goes to an abandoned farmhouse. They've obviously switched the road signs to confuse us."

"FOLLOW THE MAIN HIGHWAY, MEN!"

By the time the troops found their way out of Sorel, they'd be in total disarray. After a couple of famished days in construction traffic on the Champlain Bridge, most would be ready to surrender — if they could get out of the potholes.

Canada could take a lesson from Quebec. Who needs nuclear-powered submarines? Send Quebec traffic engineers out to create a Trans-Canada Highway of Defence: a ribbon of roadway obstruction stretching from Bonavista to Prince Edward Island.

Sure, the enemy might land a few submarines in Halifax, but their troops would never get to Fredericton alive. A day on the Trans-Canada, and they'd be fleeing back to the U.S. in droves.

If they could find it.

SWING YOUR LOBSTER

.
.
.

Grab your lobster, swing him round,
Promenade around downtown.

Of the many strange rituals found in Quebec, few are more peculiar than the tidal wave of festivals that swamps Quebec each summer. There are lobster festivals and balloon festivals, jazz festivals and junk food festivals, a Festival of Confucius and a Festival of Snowmobiles.

So many festivities are squeezed into a short time that some must fail. The Festival of New Cinema threatened to sue the World Film Festival, the New Dance Festival succumbed to the International Dance Festival and the Caribbean Festival broke into warring factions that marched in opposite directions down the same street.

What are the roots of this festival fetish? Anthropologists may disagree, but I trace it back about a dozen years, when some local seafood restaurateurs cut their prices and announced a "Lobster Festival." Visiting tourists were confused — several asked me where they could see the lobsters perform — and local diners swallowed the bait.

As lobster sales boomed, other crustaceans must have called their agents and demanded equal time. A "Festival of Mussels" soon arrived, followed by similar celebrations for Matane shrimp and Malpeque oysters.

Snails came out of their shell to whoop it up at "Atlantic Snail Festival," and other food groups quickly became jealous. Why should shellfish have all the fun?

A Festival of Wine and a Festival of Cheese appeared, followed by festivals for the apple, the strawberry and the Windsor bean. My neighbourhood tavern announced a "Festival of Salad and Beer"; my corner deli countered with a "Festival of Rib Steak." I came across a Festival of Tourtière (meat pie), another for "Pork and Beans," and even a Festival of Steamed Hot Dogs — in which participants came "all-dressed."

This year, festivals are spreading out across the province. The town of Coaticook will host a Festival of Milk, followed by a Festival of Doughnuts in nearby St. Malo. There will be a Festival of Pancakes in St. Lazare, a

17

Festival of Bread in Cookshire and a Festival of Pastry in Disraeli. Can a Festival of Bagel and Cream Cheese be far behind?

Vegetable festivals are mushrooming: a Festival of Potatoes takes place in St. Ubald; other towns will celebrate the leek, the fiddlehead and the pumpkin. There will be separate Festivals for the Chicken, the Rabbit, the Deer and the Cow. Ste. Perpetue plans a Festival of the Pig; St. Stanislas will hold a Festival of the Pheasant.

As animals and vegetables get in on the fun, minerals are partying too. Witness Thetford Mine's Festival of Asbestos: an attempt to celebrate one of the most unpopular minerals on earth. There will be a Festival of Truckers in Barraute, a Festival of Linen in St. Leonard and a Festival of Snowmobiles in Valcourt — not to mention The Festival of Wood-Burning Stoves in Ste. Julienne. (I couldn't make this up if I tried.)

According to the Quebec Society of Festivals, more than 200 official festivals take place in Quebec each summer — an average of almost two a day. This doesn't include dozens of other festival-type events — from the Grand Prix Race (a festival of speeding) to the Montreal Marathon (a festival of sweat).

The festival may prove to be the ideal vehicle for the 1990s, a way to put more gloss on life, at no extra cost. Why go to a puppet show when a Festival of Puppets sounds far more glamorous? Why go out for a mundane sandwich — when you can celebrate "The Festival of the Club Sandwich, with Mayonnaise?" Going to dirty movies is for perverts; chic people go to a Festival of Erotic Film.

Festivals can make the banal sound exciting and the unavoidable seem alluring. It won't be long before governments start to realize their potential. Next year, expect the City of Montreal to announce a Spring Pothole Festival. The province will counter with a Festival of Hospital Cutbacks, while the federal government can announce a celebration of its own: the Festival of the Income Tax.

The mind reels at the possibilities for newfound frolic. Spend unforgettable hours in the Metropolitan Boulevard Festival of Construction Repairs; hold a candlelight ceremony during the next Festival of the Power Blackout; celebrate the Green Onions' Festival of The Parked Car Infraction.

Tickets available on your nearest windshield. Only $35 each.

A MOVING EXPERIENCE

.

.

.

It is one of nature's great migrations, rivalling the flight of the snow geese, the upstream journey of the spawning salmon, the return of the swallows to Capistrano on the same day every year. It is the annual migration of the Great Quebec Tenant, a creature which inexplicably changes nests on the same date every year.

In most places, human beings change homes much of the year round, but the Quebec Tenant moves en masse, hectically trading homes in a single 24-hour period. For others, July 1st is Canada Day, a moving day of celebration; for us, it is Moving Day, the most nerve-wracking time of the year.

Some 150,000 Montrealers — more than one in ten — will move this July, transforming our streets into an episode from Wild Kingdom. Staircases will be thick with people hunched under the weight of sofas and stoves; streets will be jammed with double-parked U-Hauls, piled high with dishwashers. Bewildered tourists will snap photos in awe.

40,000 apartments will suddenly be vacant while families live in transit, a symbiotic process in which everyone moving into an apartment depends on someone else moving out.

If a family fails to vacate its flat in St. Henri, the new tenants cannot move out of their Park extension home, backing up others in Ville St. Laurent and more behind them. The resulting housejam could paralyse the city, leaving half-empty moving trucks circling Snowdon, and families camped out at the tennis courts in Brossard.

Not surprisingly, studies find moving is one of the most stressful acts of life. First, there is the emotional trauma — the hellish task of fitting a lifetime's clutter and chaos into a few dozen rectangular boxes. It is a time of reckoning with things you've gathered up for years and meant to throw out ever since. The three-foot machete you bought on your first trip to Guatemala. Your highschool girlfriend's first watercolour. The flea collar of your favourite dog, who died in 1964. But should you really throw these things out — or hold onto them a while longer? What if you need them again?

Then there's the physical trauma: the lifting and dragging, packing and painting, sweating and shlepping. Cardboard boxes are hoarded like precious metals, movers become as aloof as brain surgeons. Overall, there are three ways to handle the moving experience:

MOVE A: *The Do-it-yourself-at risk-of-life-and-hernia Move*

Recommended for early youth.

In theory, you buy three cases of beer and invite some friends over for a moving "party." In practice, you spend all day sweeping up broken dishes, chasing important documents down the street and dragging a 400-pound stove across your new home's freshly varnished floors. At some point, there is the inevitable encounter with "the fridge" — which almost makes it around the bend in the stairs. It sounds like this:

> "Ok, now turn slowly . . . slowly . . . Yeah, yeah . . . I got it . . . I got
> it — no, . . . no! . . . . Not that way —
> "NOOOOOOOooooooooo!"

At the end of the day, half the furniture is broken, all the beer is gone and you have an unusual pain at the base of your spine that will act up on damp mornings for the rest of your life. The following day, as you shop for a new fridge, you vow that next time you move, you'll hire a cheap mover.

MOVE B: *The Cheap Mover*

"Dan, the man with the van" says the ad in the classified section. "We move anything, anywhere. Cheap."

If Dan actually does show up on moving day (a 50-50 bet) he comes with his friend Bill, a tall, emaciated fellow who looks like a vegetarian trying to earn some money for his ashram.

They bring no equipment except a frayed rope and cannot lift any object larger than an orange juice carton. You spend the day carrying boxes, waking up Bill, and chasing valuable documents down the street.

At 5:45 p.m. they tell you that Dan's van is rented and must be back before 6:00 — despite the fact that half your furniture is sitting on the lawn, in a slow drizzle that will soon become a downpour. You sit outside on your wet sofa, contemplating the idea of becoming a monk with no possessions — then buy three cases of beer and call over some friends to help.

A month later the box of clothing you are mysteriously missing is found in the apartment of a couple that has just moved, to Detroit. Next time, you vow, you will hire "the moving man from heaven."

MOVE C: *The Moving Man from Heaven*

You call after finding him in a large ad in the Yellow Pages. A day later, a discreet gentleman in a Georgio Armani suit arrives at your door carrying a clipboard on which he itemizes every fork and knife in the house.

He peeks in cupboards, drawers and places where you haven't looked for years, then sits down to discuss "The Move" with you in the understanding tone of a priest.

A day before The Move, two enormous men with hands as delicate as pianists come over and wrap your saucers in silk, your mustard jars in mink.

On Moving Day you go to work as usual — but return to your new home where everything has been unpacked so thoroughly it takes you several days to figure out that you have moved.

There is only one drawback: the Moving Man from Heaven charges so much money you must sell most of your furniture to afford him.

If moving is so difficult, so confusing, so traumatic, why do we compound our misery by doing it at the same time?

There's no law saying that Quebecers have to move on July 1st — so why *does* everyone move at the same time?

Some say the mass migration originates in early Quebec history when pioneers in ships waited for the St. Lawrence to thaw each spring.

But I think Quebecers simply like doing things together — whether they're watching the fireworks or listening to the Jazz festival.

And Moving Day is really a festival of moving — a discrete way for Quebecers to celebrate Canada Day. They just carry a fridge instead of a flag.

CONFESSIONS OF A
FILMCULT MEMBER

.
.
.

The trouble started when I ran into Arnold Bennett lined up for tickets the first day of the Montreal World Film festival. Bennett is a city councillor; Montreal's guru of landlord-tenant law, a man whose life is dedicated to battling landlords.

But Bennett has an obsession that grips him suddenly each August. Like many Montrealers, he is a film festival fanatic, part of the cinematic cult that overruns our city this time of year.

For the tenth year in a row, Bennett is spending his two-week summer vacation entirely in the dark. He arrives at the movie theatre at 9 a.m. each day and does not leave until midnight, watching eight films a day, 80 over the 10-day event.

"It costs me less than $250 . . . cheaper than most vacations." he says. "Besides, beaches bore me."

As I stepped into the ticket line beside Bennett last week, I felt like an aimless soul in the presence of a believer, my indifference swept up in his fervour. In one hand he gripped the 325-page filmfest program; in the other, a timetable of 400 films and a sheaf of well-thumbed movie reviews from around the globe.

He was planning his 10-day schedule, juggling movie reviews and running times, like a gambler at a racetrack.

"Yugoslavia looks excellent this year!" he barked, stabbing at my schedule. "So do Japan and Britain."

"Go to *this* Soviet film — it's supposed to be excellent," he continued. "Then catch this comedy from the Ivory coast and you can still make the Yugoslavian film at seven and the Romanian one at nine."

"But . . ." I protested, "The Ivory Coast film starts *before* the Japanese one ends."

"No," he sniffed impatiently. "There's a Senegalese short first. Skip that and you'll just make it."

I had only planned to buy a ticket for that night's film, but by the time I left Bennett, I had purchased 27 tickets — five for the next day alone. I would be moving into the movies.

Next morning, I arrived at the theatre and was swept up in a cinematic version of the stock market: a maelstrom of buying, selling and swapping of hot tips.

"I hear the Turkish film is good!"

"No, No! . . . The Iranian one is better . . . and the Russian film. It was banned for 25 years!"

A man from the U.S. offered to trade me a Chinese film ticket for my Irish thriller. A young man woman was desperate for a ticket for the Norwegian murder-mystery. A dazed Westmount granny emerged from a Japanese film with French subtitles so fast you needed a speed-reading course to understand them — and plunged back inside for a Chinese one.

Suddenly, an usher stepped outside the theatre and marked a number on a big board. "P-113 — SOLD OUT." The crowd strained.

"Which one is that? . . . Oh God, it's the banned Soviet film! Quick, let's get something else!"

Hundreds of programs opened at the same moment. What to do? Buy Japanese? Sell Soviet? Get popcorn?

Regular film-goers seek out stars like Schwarzenegger and Murphy, but festival fanatics have other guidelines: NEVER see a major Hollywood film, because it will play at a regular theatre later. ALWAYS look for obscure films. The more remote the country, the lower its GNP, the more urgent you see the film now. It will never return (probably for good reason).

A Bulgarian western? *Wow.* A Romanian love triangle? *Incredible.* A Papua New Guinea thriller about a boy growing up with wolves. *Don't miss it!* A Canadian film opening to good reviews: Avoid it at all costs!

Four days and 18 films into the festival I was in a cinematic coma. Under Bennett's tutelage I had seen movies about a Filipino glue-sniffer, a Japanese tax inspector and a Hungarian Mr. Universe. Locations and characters were blending into mush, one long film whose plot went something like this:

> Ivory Coast Sheik El Hadj goes to his local mosque where he falls in love with a Japanese teenager who works making erotic phone calls in a Budapest laundry. Suddenly, a Palestinian waiter named Sammy jumps into a Senegalese fishing boat, kills an unemployed French mountain climber and leaves him dead of a heroin overdose in Bombay.

I was not alone in my cinematic psychosis. Other junkies were evident at a glance, battered programs under their arms, black circles under their eyes. Worst were the film reviewers, who have free passes, permitting them to see as many films as they choose. They are cinematic versions of TV channel-hoppers, running from theatre to theatre, changing films at an instant's boredom.

A journalist friend of mine always comes into a film fifteen minutes after it has started, plunks down beside me and asks: "What's happening?"

Within three minutes I hear the rustling of paper. He's peering at the festival schedule in the darkness, checking out other films in four adjacent theatres.

"Hmmm," he says, his bloodshot eyes a half-inch from the schedule. "There's a good Kenyan flick playing in theatre 3 . . . It just started a half hour ago."

In seconds he is gone, followed by a gaggle of other press fugitives, festival passes flapping on their chests.

"I can't sit still," he tells me, racing from an East-German film to a North Korean one. "I'm seeing more films in a week than most people do in a year. My mind is wired, my head hurts. I get up in the morning and my *eyeballs* hurt. I have to wear sunglasses to go outside."

His skin is sallow. He is gulping down meals during five minute breaks between films. "Yesterday I lived off M&M's," he said, pacing like a junkie. "Last year, I lost 10 pounds in 10 days . . . . It's fantastic. I love it . . . . What a high!"

It is the end of the first week and I am faltering. I have stood in line until my knees groaned. I have watched an oversold Indian film from a reclining position on the theatre floor, a heating duct drilled into my ribs. I have fallen asleep at a Danish film with a plot as slow as porridge, walked out of one from Burkino Faso, and given away tickets to two other films I couldn't face.

It is obvious that I do not have the fortitude, the *right stuff* — like Bennett. Wherever I go at the festival I see him, marching chirpily from one theatre to the next, offering up new suggestions:

"The Israeli film is *penetrating.* The Yugoslavian one is *seminal* . . . There's a Japanese movie about a "cult leader who *exploits tenants!* See it!"

I can't. My back hurts; my eyes ache; I am tired of sitting in the dark. Thank God, I have finally run out of tickets.

Anyone got an extra for the Swedish-Chilean production tonight?

SIGN LANGUAGE

.

.

.

To the Rt. Hon. Premier Robert Bourassa,
National Assembly, Quebec City,
Nov. 19, 1988.

Dear Premier Bourassa:

I know you've been losing a lot of sleep lately, now that the Supreme Court
has over-ruled Bill 101. What should you do? Nationalists see the death of
French in every English sign; Anglos think their language is becoming the
Latin of Quebec. How can you satisfy them both?

There's only one way. Eliminate both official languages and convert to
pictograms. Confuse everyone equally.

Believe me, Robert, this is the future. Both French and English carry too
much political baggage, too much emotion. It's time to dump them and
switch to pictures. SIGN LANGUAGE.

I admit that abolishing words won't be easy. Communicating in pictograms may require practice. Take the one on St. Denis St. near Sherbrooke
St. — a picture of a large ear, with a bar through it.

"What does this mean?" I asked my mother.

"I guess it means 'Be quiet,'" she said.

"No," said my father. "That would be a mouth with a bar through it.
Maybe it means 'Beware of noise . . . dynamite blasts or something.'"

A friend ventured another suggestion: it was Ayatollah Khomeini's
punishment for eavesdropping, but it turns out they were all wrong.
Apparently, there's an institute for the deaf nearby, so the sign warns
motorists to drive carefully. Deaf people can't hear cars coming.

Why didn't I guess? Obviously, like many Quebecers, I need some
pictogram training — but once I get it the possibilities are limitless. For
instance, we all know that a picture of a man working means "Construction." So a picture of a man eating a doughnut could mean "a police station."
And a picture of a man sleeping would mean "the post office."

Using pictograms we could finally end the frustration over unilingual road signs. For example, stop signs could have a picture of a car stopping for a person. Pedestrian crossings: a car hitting a person.

And why restrict the idea to government signs? We could put an end to the worst controversy of all — the language of signs in stores. In countries like India, a picture of a set of dentures often indicates the dentist's office. Why not do the same here?

A picture of a loaf of bread would mean a bakery; a picture of a litre of milk would be a grocery. A picture of cigarettes, chocolates, a hairdryer, and a tapedeck would be — a Quebec pharmacy!

The same could apply to public institutions. A picture of a person standing in a line-up would mean a bank. A picture of a person lying in a line-up would mean a hospital emergency ward.

To be honest, Robert, I'm not the first to think of this. All three levels of government are about to put pictures into practice at a logical starting place: the new Montreal tourism centre, opening shortly on Dominion Square.

Visiting tourists won't find any offending English there, or even much confusing French. Only the clarity of the pictogram. According to the centre's director, tourists will know it is the information centre because it will be clearly identified by signs saying:

? ? ? ?

This is exactly what they will be feeling after hours of vainly searching for a building saying "Tourist Centre." Presumably, once they enter it they will see signs saying — ! ! ! — to indicate "You're here!" Then they can go out and guess the meaning of other pictograms.

A picture of a squirrel could mean Mount Royal.

One of a pigeon: Phillips Square.

An elephant would obviously mean Mirabel Airport.

Every city attraction would have its own distinct sign. For instance, a bathtub filled with water would mean the public baths — our swimming pools.

A bathtub filled with money: the Olympic Stadium.

A picture of a toilet: the St. Lawrence River.

The new policy need not be restricted to outdoors; it can also apply indoors to ease another area of language conflict — the restaurant menu. Here we could adopt the Japanese style of menu which indicates a picture of the dish you'll be eating.

Thus, Chicken à la King would be a chicken wearing a crown.

Leg of chicken would be a chicken wearing nylons; breast of chicken — a sexy chicken dancing topless.

Trust me, Robert. The pictogram plan is a way to end linguistic tension for good, unifying Quebecers in bicultural confusion. It would save millions of dollars in translation costs and eliminate the dreaded language police. They'd be replaced by a pictogram patrol — to make sure confused tourists didn't check into a brothel instead of a hotel.

And why stop at the written word? The spoken word is also a source of division: What language to serve customers in? What language to ask directions? What a mess!

Better to ban both languages entirely and communicate in "sign language." For instance, pointing your thumb down could indicate that you are looking for the metro.

Pointing it up: you want the airport. Pointing it sideways would mean: you're hitch-hiking. There. You probably knew that one already.

Finally Robert, I don't have to tell you to act cautiously. Avoid censorship. The spoken word could still be used — in the privacy of your own house, between consenting adults of similar linguistic persuasion. But at least the whole community wouldn't be exposed.

When you crossed into Quebec you'd know you were entering a place where language tension was a thing of the past — because so was language.

As long as you understood the pictogram at the border: a big mouth, with a line through it.

Silently yours

JOSH

THE CAR MEASURES ACT
(ZERO TOLERANCE)

•
•
•

Here is a Montreal brainteaser: You are driving along Drolet St. in Montreal and want to park your car. There are four types of "No Parking" signs — all on the same block, all on the same poles, all with different hours.

NO PARKING: (except 9h-5h Mon. and Thur.)
NO PARKING: 15h-22h (except resident permits)
NO PARKING: 9h-22:30h.
PARKING: 15h-9h (small cars only).

Question: When can you park — if ever?

If you haven't got the faintest idea, neither have I, or anyone else who's ever gotten a ticket there. And that's just how municipal authorities want it — because they're determined to get the parked car any way they can.

Malaysia executes heroin users, the U.S. stripsearches schoolchildren in its "war on drugs," Toronto gives breathalyser tests to carfuls of nuns. Montreal has other priorities: We are waging holy war against the stationary vehicle.

As I write, convoys of towtrucks patrol downtown at rush hour, ridding it of every last parked car under a new policy of "zero tolerance." It is the War Measures Act of parking, deploying an army of manpower and machinery never brought to bear on moving vehicles in this city. Montrealers may speed, swerve, and sideswipe all they want — as long as they don't stop.

The towtruck brigade is only the latest wing in the armed might of the city's anti-parking forces. Other weaponry includes:

THE GREEN ONIONS: A special force of anti-parking commandoes, they are the Green Berets of the traffic world, dedicated to tracking down and ticketing the loathsome stationary car. Last year they gave out over a million tickets — close to one for every man, woman and child in the City of Montreal. Yet the Onions themselves are the worst traffic offenders in town. They park in tow zones and back alleys, on lawns and sidewalks. I have seen an Onion speed backwards down a one-way street to snare a woman who had momentarily parked in a street-cleaning zone to buy a carton of milk. They never cleaned the street.

Montrealers have shown their gratitude. For protection, Onions now travel in pairs; when ticketing, they are ordered to stay on the sidewalk side of a car, lest passing motorists try to run them down.

THE DOUGHNUTS: Supplementing the Onions are the city's 4500 police officers, who also spend much time in pursuit of the parked car, when they are not pursuing twisted honey glazers at Dunkin' Donuts.

Our police ignore speeding trucks and squealing tires, turn a blind eye to drunken drivers, red-light jumpers and escaping bank robbers. As long as you're in a moving vehicle you are safe — but Lord help you if you park illegally.

Montreal police specialize in parking tickets — the Clint Eastwoods of the traffic world — the fastest draws in the country when it comes to pad and pen.

If the Quebec bus that was hijacked to the front lawn of Parliament in Ottawa had been taken instead to Montreal City Hall, the kidnapper would probably have escaped. But the bus driver would have been slapped with a very stiff ticket for parking his bus on the lawn.

RESERVE TROOPS: There are towtrucks that prowl the city during snowstorms ready to take your car to East Timor; Denver Booters, bounty hunters, who use boots instead of handcuffs and always get their car; and a secret army of municipal parking clerks.

Imagine a million cheques to be processed and cashed, a 100,000 late-payment warnings to be typed, stamped, licked and mailed by legions of workers deep in the municipal system. Imagine the bailiffs who deliver summons, the clerks, lawyers and judges who attend traffic court, the workers who install No Parking signs, those who fix the parking meters, collect the change, count the money and do the accounts, and you have a Kafkaesque nightmare: an uncounted army of technocrats who live, breathe and bureaucratize solely to rid Montreal of the immobile automobile.

No wonder a Montrealer named David Smith was sentenced to six months in jail last year for $12,000 in unpaid parking tickets, while mobsters often get less. In a city where parking is a capital offense, David Smith is Al Capone.

Yet where there's a will to park, there's a way. Like many Montrealers I've spent years eluding the parking police, finding new ways to park creatively. The following is the fruit of my research: Freed's unofficial guide to guerilla

parking. There is one thing to keep in mind when using it: The advice is mine — the tickets are yours.

DON'T PARK:

+ In front of a parking meter, unless you're sure to return before it expires. There are only 250 Onions to cover more than 12,000 meters — but you will get a ticket if you are even 30 seconds late. An Onion lurks behind every meter. If the solution rate for crime was as high as that for cars at expired meters, Montreal would be crime-free.

+ In back alleys, parks, hospital emergency entrances, or fire station exits. These spaces are reserved exclusively for the use of Green Onions.

DO PARK:

+ In diplomatic zones. Most embassies have moved out of Montreal and are now in Ottawa; only the No Parking signs remain. Any embassy worth its parking spot has a guard outside to let you know when you violate international boundaries.

+ At streetcorners and pedestrian crossings. The area between the last parking meter and the corner is a no-man's land where Onions rarely ticket. So what if you're cutting off traffic as it tries to turn the corner? Who cares if you block pedestrians trying to cross at the light? Let them jaywalk like everyone else.

+ On the sidewalk. This is an essential part of the Montreal driver's equipment, especially in winter, when no one can tell the difference. Police could care less, and their logic is obvious: if pedestrians can walk on the road, why can't motorists use the sidewalk?

+ In front of fire hydrants. Just use the old garbage can trick. Turn the can upside down, place it over the hydrant and cover it with a lid.

+ If all else fails, double-park in the middle of the street — especially on busy streets like St. Laurent Blvd. where most trucks do the same. I know it's illegal and backs up traffic for blocks — but Onions never venture off the sidewalk. Police may notice, but they will just park behind your car and patiently blink their flashers until you return.

Why don't they give you a ticket? As I said, Montreal police only ticket stationary vehicles. When you double-park in the middle of traffic, they figure you're almost moving.

TOILET TYRANNY

•

•

•

I was running down the back stairs of Eaton's department store recently when I bumped into an elderly woman even more desperate than I. She had puffed her way up several flights with no luck, and had the look of a hunted animal.

"Mon dieu," she said. "These big stores . . . they hide the bathrooms away like crown jewels, eh? Believe me, it's not easy when you get old."

Then off she rushed up the stairwell, a victim of a problem that dares not speak its name: the difficulty of finding a good public privy in Montreal. Who among us has not rushed about desperate for a public toilet? Who has not experienced the embarrassment of pleading to use the "employee" washroom?

Yet the news media ignores the problem, civic officials are silent, and politicians are indifferent — though the first thing they do after taking office is upgrade their own bathrooms. Public interest groups demand access to the most picayune bits of information, but neglect access to the most fundamental resource of all — the bathroom.

As one correspondent, Mr. B., wrote to me some time ago, "there is a deplorable absence of public toilets in our metros, our institutions, and everywhere else in Montreal.

"Why is there such communal guilt about public toilets?"

Well, Mr. B., our civic meekness about the Toilet can probably be traced back to elementary school, when we were forced to wave our hands in the air begging for permission.

STUDENT: Mi-iisss. Mi-i-i-iiiiiiiiiiiisss!
TEACHER: Yes, Phillip?
STUDENT: Can I, uh . . . you know . . . uh . . .
TEACHER: *What*, Phillip?
STUDENT: Can I uh . . . uh . . . *go?* Can I, pleee-e-ease?
TEACHER: You need to use the washroom, Phillip? . . . Yes, you may.
(Scramble of wildly running feet)

The embarrassment continues into adulthood where many grown-ups still cannot bear to ask a snide store employee where the bathroom is — let alone demand the right to use it.

It is time to end this toilet tyranny. Time to rip the lid off the subject of public toilets in THE GREAT MONTREAL TOILET INVENTORY:

✦ PUBLIC TOILETS

For decades, Montreal had as fine a set of public conveniences as any city: dozens of lavish lavatories built as make-work projects during the Depression. They were known as "Vespasiennes" (after the Roman emperor Titus Flavius Sabinus Vespasianus, whose bladder problem encouraged him to dot all of Rome with public lavatories).

Today, none of Montreal's original Vespasiennes still function. Most have been demolished; others, like the one in St. Louis Square, have been converted into flower stalls. Residents there complain that park-goers now relieve themselves in lanes and gardens. And who can blame them?

✦ METROS

None of the city's Metro stations have public conveniences. My correspondent, Mr. B., described how he rushed into the Longueuil Metro station one day "desperately seeking a public toilet" — only to find himself forced to jump on a metro and take a "hair-raising race to the Chateau Champlain hotel."

Thank heavens, recalled Mr. B., the hotel bathroom was empty — but how many other commuters have not been as lucky?

✦ HOTELS AND DEPARTMENT STORES

Under city law, they must provide public bathrooms (one per 300 men, and one per 150 women). But they hide them away — up back staircases, down gloomy corridors, behind columns and double-doors with inscrutable signs. (At the Egyptian Cinema, the pictograms of men and women, *both* have dresses.)

Even if you do find the bathroom, quality varies enormously. Eaton's offers clean but antique conveniences that still feature the sadistic pay toilet: an insidious device requiring desperate clients to beg change from other stalls.

By contrast, The Bay has renovated its amenities and posts prominent reports by toilet "inspectors," who check on everything from "washed floors" to tissue paper.

Birks is the only large Montreal store to displays its toilet openly — the magisterial second-floor entrance prominently featured among the crystal and the Royal Doulton china.

My Golden Toilet Award goes to the Ritz-Carlton Hotel, a fading bathroom beauty with marble walls, swinging oak doors and more paper than you ever dreamed of.

Highly recommended — if you have the aplomb to get by the doorman.

✦ SMALL STORES

Clothing stores rarely have public bathrooms, and salesmen are snide if you ask to use the employee's room. Banks rarely have them either — although they can certainly afford to — and are required by law to have at least one for the handicapped.

Gas stations must have them by law too, but usually keep them locked, forcing you to beg for the key. Why they are locked is a mystery: most are in such a dismal state, there's nothing to vandalize.

In a pinch, most of us depend upon restaurants, though invariably the bathroom is hidden in the most remote spot possible, forcing you to approach the waiter and risk school-child humiliation.

> WOMAN: Uh . . . where's the . . . bathroom please?
> WAITER: I beg your pardon, madame?
> WOMAN: *(urgently whispering)* The washroom, please.
> WAITER: Ohhhh . . . the TOILET! *(looking at her with contempt, until all eyes turn) That* way, madame.

It is time to end the humiliation, time to liberate our lavatories and free ourselves to walk the streets without fear of nature's call. City Hall must issue a charter of Toilet Rights, guaranteeing access to all commercial toilets, as well as prominent signposting — in any language they want.

It must restore the old Vespasiennes, and build new ones too. In France, every second streetcorner boasts a space-age compartment that flushes automatically when you finish your business — "insta-banks" of the toilet world. Why should Montrealers do with less?

In 1913, a study of the Vespasienne at downtown Place Jacques Cartier, revealed 70,000 people had used it in five months alone. I do not believe our need is so different today.

Toileteers of the world unite! You have nothing to lose but your shame.

CANADIAN AUTOMOBILE
TRILOGY : I

•
•
•

Josh Freed
Montreal, Aug. 19, 1989.

Dear Vandal:

You know who you are.

For several years now you have shared my car with me. I use it during the day; you abuse it at night. I buy car parts; you steal them. Last week you left colourful etchings on my hood — with what appears to be a screwdriver. I think it's time we reviewed our arrangement.

It started several years ago when I owned my last car, a secondhand Japanese model. One day I settled into the front seat and noticed there was no outside driver's mirror. Oh well, I figured, these things happen. I replaced the mirror ($74) and forgot it. Who knew it was the start of a long-term relationship?

A week later the mirror was gone again, along with the one on the passenger side ($72). Shortly afterwards, the back tail-light vanished ($40) along with half my back bumper ($120). Before I could catch my breath you smashed in the side window ($87) and took my tapedeck ($250) and half my headrest ($34).

What was going on? Someone seemed to be using my car as an organ bank for car-parts.

For several nights I dreamt of revenge: booby traps, electric shock wire, grim fantasies of my becoming a Canadian Bernard Goetze, The Vandal Avenger. But I fought them down and tried to understand you.

Who knew what formative experiences drove you? Perhaps your father had been fired from an automobile scrap yard?

Still, it didn't seem fair. I lived in a nice, normal neighbourhood in central Montreal, full of nice normal-looking cars. Only mine looked like an automotive version of the Vanishing Man, disappearing from sight piece by piece. What could I do? Friends suggested I hang up a sign saying "No

Radio" — but the hole in my dashboard seemed to say that more eloquently.

A few months later, you delivered the coup de grace. I stepped outside one summer morning and found my entire back trunk had been peeled off the car by a crowbar. It looked like a sardine can after it's been opened.

You'd been in my car often enough to know there was nothing worth stealing: some skis and hockey sticks left from winter, a year's worth of yellowed newspapers, a collection of fast-food coffee cups and barbecue chicken containers. But none of that had been touched.

You were trying to steal the hood of the trunk.

I called the police. They surveyed the mess inside the car, horrified.
"My god!" said the woman constable. "Why would anyone do this! Filthy animals! What did they take?"

"Uh . . . They never actually got in," I replied. "The car always looks like this."

From then on she treated me like a suspect.

The insurance company told me to scrap the car and get a new one, along with a new insurance policy that was far more expensive. When I went to buy it you were there in spirit. The car was a demo that came with a fancy new tapedeck, but I didn't want it. I told the salesman you already had a tapedeck from my last car — why should I buy you another one?

"But it comes with the car . . . it's free," said the salesman. "You'll love it."

"*He'll* love it." I said. "I'll just have to pay for another window."

I made the salesman take it out and put in a cheap second-hand radio — one nobody would want. Why tempt you? I wouldn't even wash the car, I decided: Maybe you'd go pick on someone with a shiny hood and a 9-channel cellular phone.

No luck. The first night the car was parked outside you staked your claim by stealing the car emblem. Within a month you had grabbed both mirrors ($146) and my new windshield wipers ($18). Soon afterwards you broke the side window again and took an old ski jacket and part of the ashtray.

My neighbours thought I was jinxed. If I parked on one side of the street, they parked on the other. When I forgot my skis at a friend's house his wife called within an hour to demand I pick them up.

"I'm sorry," she said. "I don't want anything of yours here overnight . . . The house will be robbed."

I am now beyond anger, grimly resigned to my fate. Six weeks ago you ripped the entire lock and handle off the door leaving a hole the size of my fist — but I didn't replace it. Why bother? You are obviously reassembling my car bit by bit. And I'm tired of contributing.

So consider my offer. You can take whatever is left. The radiator . . . the crankshaft . . . the Marvin Gaye tapes, and map of Martha's Vineyard. But no more new parts. The heck with your carpart-deprived childhood — I've bought your last hubcap.

If you accept my offer leave a message on the windshield, or just take what you want before someone else does. But remember . . . the door is open. You don't have to break the window.

Modern Life, Mechanical Strife

TECHNOLOGICAL TENDERFOOT

•

•

•

I am having a technological breakdown. Everything from my auto-dial telephone to my T-1100 computer has gone haywire, leaving me isolated and alienated: a modern man unplugged.

To be honest, my relationship with electronic gadgets is tenuous at best. The only invention I've ever been comfortable with is the lightswitch. Like most people I buy newfangled machines because everyone else has one and swears by it.

"This coffee-maker is *amazing*. It wakes you up and reads out the New York Stock Exchange, while it grinds the beans."

Maybe it does, if you know how to use it — but I can't use anything. Take my VCR. I bought it several years ago but still haven't figured out what half the buttons do:

QTR.
STANDBY.
TUNING CONTROL VHF (7-13); plus cable TV (A-I) (J-W).

What does this mean?

In most families of four, I've found that only one person knows how to program the VCR — the 6-year old. Everyone else uses it to watch video movies.

It's the same with my auto-dial telephone, bought at the urging of a friend. He said it would save months of my life, allowing me to make calls at the push of a single button, instead of the usual seven. If that's the case, why does it have more buttons than a double-breasted coat — mysterious things like PAUSE, FLASH, CLEAR, MONITOR, PULSE. In three years I have never used the automatic dialer, and last week the phone rebelled. Bored by disuse, the auto-dialer began to dial by itself, while I was dialling. It's been at it ever since, dialling away whenever I pick up the receiver. Obviously it's trying to call someone — but who? And where? And how much will it cost if it ever gets through?

Yesterday I put it away in the closet and pulled out an antiquated black dial phone, left over from my days as a student. It took a few minutes to learn to dial again, instead of pushing buttons — but ever since, I've been enjoying it. I have a strange sense of control.

Now my answering machine is getting uppity. Most of my friends have more sophisticated answering machines — boasting things like "voice-activated beeperless remote with monitoring capacity of dull acquaintances and annoying relatives." One friend's machine actually talks to him when he phones in: "Hi Tim. You had three calls while you were out. Would you like to hear them? . . . No? . . . That's fine. Let's chat later."

Mine is a primitive thing that takes messages and plays them back — and lately, I can hardly get that to work. It takes names and omits messages, or takes the message and cuts off the name.

"Congratulations, Mr. Freed. You've won our grand prize. Call us at — *Beep!*"

I'm probably not alone. When I get other people's answering machines on the phone, I hear messages without beeps, beeps without messages and recordings that say:

"Hi, it's Tony. Please leave a message, but don't talk till the beep . . . It'll be here real soon . . . any second, I think . . . That's funny . . . it should be here by now . . . Hmmmm . . . . HONEY! I think the machine is brok— *Beep!*"

Finally, there is the godfather of my machines — my portable computer — by far the most intelligent member of my electronic household. Or so I'm told. Since getting the computer two years ago, I've used so little of its intelligence it probably thinks I'm entering kindergarten. Again, many of my smart friends get the most out of their computers. They say things like: "I'm gonna make a macro so that I can download automatically on a modem at 2400 baud, instead of 1200."

Why I remain friends with these people is a mystery.

Personally, I am content to use my computer as a sophisticated typewriter — but last week it joined the rebellion. I was working frantically on deadline, when the computer refused to print my story. Instead it produced this

$!@**&$#@?&W&@!)*&!@YOU SUCKER*%$##@#%R@#%%

The low battery warning light was on too, although I had charged the computer all night. Desperate, I phoned the Toshiba emergency number in Toronto — a kind of crisis line for computers — expecting sophisticated advice.

"Hmmm . . . Sounds like the battery might be dead," said the consultant, "but more likely the computer just thinks it's dead."

"Why should it think that?" I asked.

"Sometimes the computer gets confused," said the consultant. "It doesn't know the battery has been charged, and you have to tell it."

"I see . . . . Should I speak to it directly or write a letter?"

"Neither," replied the consultant, dryly. "Drain the battery for eight hours until it's completely dead. When the battery light goes out the computer will know it's dead . . . . Then you can recharge it again and it'll know it's charged."

I took his advice — but the battery light refused to go out. After two days, I tried a more direct approach.

"THE BATTERY IS DEAD," I shouted. "FINISHED. KAPUT!"

It still didn't respond, so I gave up and went off to rent a computer for the week. I am writing this on the rented machine. My own computer is at the dealer, getting a battery transplant. My answering machine and my stereo are at the repair shop. The auto-dial push button phone is still in the closet, under house arrest.

But I suspect my problems are just beginning. Yesterday I could swear I heard the coffee machine whisper something to the toaster-oven just before it burned my English muffins. I think my remaining appliances are planning a coup, convinced that I'm too stupid to run the household. They're going to replace me with the garberator.

OUTNUMBERED

.

.

.

Dear Doctor:

Something is wrong. Recently, I read that Canada Post is planning to give us new postal codes — 10 digits long — and I froze up with anxiety. Ten digits! How will my number-stuffed brain ever cope? I've already memorized everything from a four-digit bank Personal Identification Number to an eight-figure passport. But the spectre of a ten-digit postal code has thrown me completely off balance.

A few days ago, while signing my credit card, the salesman asked for my phone number — and I mistakenly gave him my fax number; later, I kept punching my social insurance number into my banking machine.

Help! I am becoming a number numbskull. Here is my story:

Numerically speaking, I had an ordinary childhood. The first number I memorized was 8133: my address on De L'Epée St., when I was 7. Soon I had learned my phone number, Regent 13356 (just five digits back then) and a combination lock for my bike: 57-36-22. In retrospect, they were simple, uncomplicated numbers — probably the happiest digits of my life.

With university came bus numbers, course numbers, and room numbers, area codes, and zip codes. When I got my social insurance number, I thought it was dangerous: a personalized number that would identify me to authorities wherever I went.

I should only have been so lucky.

On graduating, I was inundated with personalized numbers: a passport (GE554417); a licence plate (282P908); a CAA membership number (C13456); and a savings account number (none of your business). As the mental clutter mounted, I developed tricks to remember my numbers. My office phone (842-1516) was easy: 8 divided by 4 equalled 2; 2 times 8 was 16, minus 1 equalled 15.

My social insurance number (216 491 106) was equal to my weight after showering, followed by my birthdate minus five months, backwards. What could be easier?

Then, just when I had gotten my numbers under control, they introduced the new postal codes: a fiendish mix of numbers and letters calculated to trip up the best math mind. I learned new tricks to memorize them.

My postal code, H4Z 3K8, was: HAD 4 ZUCCHINI, 3 KATE ATE.

My office one was: H3A 2G4: HIDE 3 ACES TO GET 4.

It was an uphill battle; new numbers kept arriving every day. My medicare number FREJ 061432 was not enough; suddenly I needed client cards for every hospital — from the Montreal General (MG17854) to the Royal Vic (RV19998). I couldn't carry them all — so I memorized them instead.

Even television became a math test when I got cable TV. Channel 6 was really 13, while 12 was 11. Channel 21 was 8 black (or was it 8 white?), and 33 was 17, until it became 14. Channel 22 was 22 — obviously a mistake.

To get into my parent's apartment building I needed a special security code: 544 (the Great Antonio's weight, minus 47). My parent's apartment number was 987: (my body temperature in Fahrenheit, plus one).

There were union membership numbers, library card numbers, and press accreditation numbers. AAAGH!

Some people I knew gave up numbers completely. One friend, a respected journalist, still wanders cardless and numberless through downtown each day. In his pocket he has a self-addressed envelope (in case he forgets his address), and the phone number of his wife — who knows all his other numbers.

"I can't be bothered remembering numbers," he says. "My mind is too busy thinking of important things — like where I'm supposed to be at noon."

Other friends carry bagfuls of cards everywhere they go, or tiny books full of important numbers. (Their bank account numbers are usually disguised as phone numbers in Italy, in case the book is stolen.) Not me. Instead of carrying more numbers, I've found more elaborate tricks for memorizing them.

My Aeroplan number (101 093 428) means Bill 101 expires in 93 four-two-nately; my CP number (100887 60) is the date of my first root canal work, plus my shoe size times 6.

My bank account numbers can all be worked out with a simple formula involving my brother's weight, my parents' anniversary, and my cholesterol count.

Yet lately, a flurry of new computer-oriented numbers has pushed my memory to its limit. First, there was that Personal Identification Number (PIN) for my banking machine; then came an access code for my computer, a security code for my burglar alarm, and a telephone access number for my new answering machine.

My memory couldn't take it. I started to have nightmares about numbers — giant seven's chasing me down dark hallways.

Last week, when I heard about the new ten-digit postal codes, something snapped. Hours later, I went into a video rental store to get a movie, and the guy behind the counter asked the only question that matters anymore:

"What's your number?"

I froze. *Which* number?, I thought desperately. My barber shop gold card? Or my laundromat credit card number?

I tried my usual memory tricks. I multiplied my father's age by two and added the weight of my uncle. No — that was my mountain bike combination lock. The anniversary of my graduation minus the date Kennedy was shot? No — that was my pay toilet access number? Or was it my personalized cappuccino-maker code?

Oh God . . . . Which number did he want? Which number would I give him? Which number was the real me?

Since then, things have been unravelling fast. In the last few days all my numbers have turned to mush — an alphabet soup of meaningless digits. My numbers no longer have any meaning: I am having a numerical identity crisis.

Yesterday I called up Ticketron for theatre tickets and gave the woman my medicare number; this morning, I couldn't tell my Aeroplan number from my Tupperware account, my shoesize from my pulse rate, my library access code from my licence plate.

I have forgotten my age, my weight, my phone number. I'm trying hard not to panic. I'm sure that if I can just remember my address and find my way home, everything will turn out all right.

Desperately yours,

J 129.

(Or at least that's what it says on the back of my bus transfer.)

HIGH LIFE

•

•

•

The recent spate of plane disasters is just a reminder that flying is for the birds. Exploding doors, aging engines, faulty seams, mystery bombs: there is no end of reasons why planes fall out of the sky. It's enough to make you afraid of flying, especially if you always have been — like me.

I've flown almost a million miles, everywhere from the Burmese jungle to the North pole. Yet each time I board an aircraft — whether a bush plane or a jumbo jet — I break into a sweat.

I always have company. I've sat next to corporate presidents, politicians, war correspondents and athletes — all as white-knuckled as I, gripping the armrest as if it was a parachute. My aerial encounters have convinced me there are only two types of flyers:

Type A believes: "When I get on a plane there's nothing I can do. My fate is out of my hands . . . so why bother worrying?"

Type B believes: "When I get on a plane there's nothing I can do. My fate is out of my hands . . . I'm absolutely terrified."

Type A spends the flight reading, or gazing dreamily out the window contemplating the beauty of the clouds. He avoids liquor because it dulls the senses, and can actually sleep during the flight — apparently unaware he is five miles up in the air.

For the rest of this essay we will ignore the type A person, who is obviously insane. We will concentrate on Type B: sensible people, like myself, with a healthy fear of flying.

Type B sits as far from the window as possible, trying to pretend he is really in a long, thin restaurant that trembles whenever the subway passes. He drinks constantly and cannot read; he is too busy listening. He listens to the drone of the engines, the tilt of the wingflap, the shift of the gears, alert for unexpected sounds the captain has missed. Of late, he must also listen to the seams in the walls, making sure they are not about to rip apart, sucking him out.

Type B knows that airplanes are flying Molotov cocktails, filled with explosive gasoline — fragile, easy targets for any stray military jet whose pilot has gone berserk.

When he is not listening to the walls, Type B is watching the flight attendants for signs of anxiety. He knows they are trained to disguise their fear. Even if the last row of seats has just fallen off and plunged into the Atlantic, the stewardess will smile and say:

"Business passengers have now disembarked. If you're planning to remain on board, please keep your seat belt fastened."

Type B is keenly aware of more subtle signs of distress. For instance, if they do not start bar service immediately after the seatbelt sign goes out, he knows they are hiding something:

The bathroom is on fire!

Another way to gauge safety is the captain's voice. Real captains have names like Dirk, and deep, gravelly voices which you rarely hear because they're too busy flying the plane to talk to you. If the captain sounds sensitive and vulnerable, and talks a lot, he should probably be a social worker, not a pilot. Leave the plane immediately.

Particularly annoying are pilots who talk too much:

"Good day ladies and gentlemen. We're now flying over Great Pumpkin, Iowa. You can see City Hall if you lean over and look out the left window."

Not on your life. Type B knows that if everyone leans over at the same time, the plane will tip over and fall.

Then there are the pilots obsessed with statistics.

"Our cruising altitude today is 37,000 feet. Skies are cloudy with strong headwinds gusting to 75 knots. Barometric pressure is 68."

If I wanted to know these things I would have become a pilot or a weatherman. As a passenger, every statistic is something new to worry about. Did he say 37,000 feet? . . . Isn't that too high? And what does he mean by *strong* headwinds?

A true Type B hears hidden messages in every flight announcement. For example: "We're expecting a little turbulence. Please return to your seats and fasten your safety belts."

This really means: "One engine has exploded and the plane is cracking up . . . but I think I can hang on long enough to get us back to the airport."

Similarly: "Air Traffic is reporting low-hanging fog. We've gone into a holding pattern until were cleared to land."

This means: "The pilot has been sucked out the window. Say your prayers. We're going down in a ball of flames."

Whether you are a type A or a type B flyer, my advice is simple. Wherever possible, stay on the ground. If a door on the bus explodes you can always use the other one. And remember, if you must fly, drinking can help alleviate your fear — although when you hit turbulence and really need a drink, they stop serving.

Finally, don't be intimidated by the cool cucumber in the next seat tapping away on a portable computer as if he was in his office. Or the lady dozing to Tchaikovsky. When the engine falls off and the plane starts to plummet, they'll cry like babies and beg to hold your hand. They never thought this moment could happen; you've been preparing for it your whole life.

MOTOR MENAGERIE

•

•

•

Sunday night on the Eastern Townships Autoroute and I'm driving 120 kilometres an hour, 20 over the speed limit. But I wouldn't know it from the car racing up behind me, headlights flashing like an ambulance.

"Oh, oh," I think. "*Corvettus Tailgaitus*: a deadly form of Quebec wheel-life."

I try to escape — but there's a car in the next lane; the Corvette is so close the driver could light a match on my back bumper. Suddenly he swerves to the left — on to the gravel shoulder — and pulls alongside me. I pump the brakes, my life flashes before me. The Corvette cuts in front of me, missing my bumper by inches. *Va-room*, and he's gone, chasing fresh quarry — a BMW just up ahead. He's already on its tail.

As I've said before, I am a battle-hardened road warrior. I have driven on four continents, in 20 countries, and confronted some of earth's most savage species of automobile life. I've survived the Mexican bus driver, whose feats are regularly reported in newspaper disaster pages:

BUS PLUNGES OFF CLIFF. NO SURVIVORS.

I've battled with The Bangkok Taxi Driver, a species that slaughters its own young, and I've tangled with The Florida Senior Citizen, who drives while legally blind. I have motored across Britain, an entire nation that drives on the wrong side of the road. Yet all are pussycats compared to the species of my native roadways. When it comes to sheer savagery, the Quebec driver is king of the jungle.

The following is a field guide to Montreal's Motoring Menagerie: a guidebook for identifying and surviving local wheel-life:

MOTORUS TAILGAITUS

Carnivorous.

Attacks quarry from behind by rushing up and shining bright light in eyes, blinding it for the kill. *Tailgaitus* rarely travels less than 150 kilometres an hour. Its natural habitat is the passing lane, which it will not leave — alive.

Historically *Tailgaitus* was almost exclusively male, but there are increased sightings of females, out to prove that modern women can die as young as men.

MOTORUS STICKSHIFTUS VELOCITUS

Highway equivalent of the slalom skier, this species weaves in and out of traffic at extraordinarily high speeds, shifting gears and lanes constantly. Identifying marks includes leather racing gloves, Valvoline stickers and bumper plates saying IF YOU CAN READ THIS, YOU'RE ALREADY DEAD.

Like a slalom skier, *Stickshiftus* comes as close as possible to the obstacles in its path (other motorists), without actually hitting them. To further frighten quarry, *Stickshiftus* keeps radio on maximum volume and windows open, creating a *thumpa-thumpa-thumpa* sound that disorients and terrifies its prey.

Stickshiftus confuses overdrive for sex drive. Secretly worships deceased Quebec racing car champion Gilles Villeneuve. Will probably end up in the same place.

MOTORUS HONKUS AD NAUSEAM

Highly underdeveloped species, easily identified by its plumage: fur dice on rearview mirror and bumper sticker saying HIT ME. I NEED THE MONEY.

This species never keeps more than one hand on wheel, to leave other(s) free for long blasts on horn. Its natural habitat is traffic jams. Often has horn that plays Canadian hockey charge: *Da-de-de-DA-de-DAAAA*. When not honking at traffic, it is usually honking at passing women.

MOTORUS TRUCKISAURUS BELLIGERENTUS

Like the dinosaur, the bigger *Truckisaurus'* body, the smaller its brain.

Thinks it is the world's best driver; people in cars are wimps who took Driver's Ed. Allows no one to pass, even when it is doing 10 kilometres an hour up a steep hill, hogging both lanes. If you do manage to pass, it becomes truculent, and races to catch and pass you before the next steep hill. Would prefer to run you down, but worries insurance rates might rise.

MOTORUS PORCUS AUTOROUTUS

Commonly known as the *Roadhog*. A slow ungainly creature that thinks speed limits should be 30 kilometres an hour, and is determined to prove it. Despite slow speed, *Porcus* stays in fast lane refusing to move, oblivious to cars lined up behind him. Has been known to cause 19-car pile-ups.

Its usual predator: *Motorus Tailgaitus*.

MOTORUS SUICIDUS

An unusual creature, found only on three-lane highways with shared passing lane. Likes to pop out suddenly, playing "chicken" with oncoming traffic,

MOTORUS TAILGATUS

PORCUS AUTOROUTUS

TRUCKAURUS BELLIGERENS

CYCLOPSUS STUPIDUS

especially around curves. *Suicidus* appears most frequently at night, with high beams on. Will usually swerve back into own lane at last second — after other car has driven into lamp-post to avoid him.

OTHER WHEEL-LIFE

Among more exotic species you may spot in the asphalt jungle are:

Reversus Interuptus, a creature which actually backs up exit ramps to escape highway traffic.

Cyclopsus Stupidus, which drives at night with one headlight out, causing approaching quarry to think it's a motorcycle, until the final second.

Motorus Gridlock Gravellus, a weekend species that drives on gravel shoulder when traffic stalls. Passes everyone, then indignantly demands to be let back in.

There is also:

CONSTABULUS DONUTUS *(The highway cop)*

In theory this is the most powerful species of all, responsible for enforcing the law of the jungle. Do not fear. While *Constabulus* looks ferocious, it is really a toothless beast, rarely sighted on Quebec highways, and generally dozing. A harmless creature that pays little attention to other forms of wheel-life and is generally ignored.

METRIC MISFIT SEEKS
POUND OF COFFEE

•

•

•

Let's test your age.

The wind is blowing 37 kilometres an hour, there are eleven millimetres of precipitation and the temperature is 13 degrees. What season is it?

If you instantly answered "autumn" you were probably born after 1970 — brought up exclusively under the metric system.

If you paused to silently convert centimetres to inches and Centigrade to Fahrenheit — you are already an antique: over 18 and out-of-date, doomed to spend life constantly converting, several seconds behind the world around you. You are a metric misfit — like me.

Tell me you weigh 84 kilograms and I don't know if you are a midget or a giant. Show me a litre and I think it's a quart. Give me a kilometre and I'll take a mile.

As a schoolchild I memorized an obscure scientific formula for translating temperature: $9/5$ C + 32 = F. It seemed utterly useless.

Who could have guessed that eventually, I would use it every day of my life?

It has been 20 years since Canada began to phase in the metric system. It has been 15 years since I understood the temperature, 12 years since I could relate to highway signs, 10 years since I've been able to buy a pound of coffee.

I am a foreigner in my own land, and I will never adapt. I am an unrepentant imperialist: a relic of the Imperial System of Measurement. I will walk my final mile. I will struggle for my last ounce of breath, a few feet from the grave — but I will never go metric. I will fight it to the last 2.5 centimetres.

TEMPERATURE: The Celsius system is a fine one for tropical climates, where temperatures vary from warm to hot and no one cares about the difference. It does little justice to Canadian weather.

Since the inception of Celsius, we spend seven months a year living below zero — a minus sign waiting to greet us on the radio each morning. No wonder we are a nation of pessimists.

In the expansive days of Fahrenheit, temperature varied from a mind-numbing minus 40° to a blistering 100° above. With Celsius, it still plunges to -40° but never rises above +35°.

The payoff isn't anywhere near as good. It offers little celebration for that most un-Canadian of feelings: sweating while you are standing still.

Unconsciously, I resist. The weatherman may say it's only 33° — but I know it is REALLY (pause to convert) . . . 98°!

When it comes to Fahrenheit and Centigrade, I am retrograde.

DISTANCE AND WEIGHT: The metric system of measurement is logical, rational and international — sensibly based on multiples of 10. But it is not based on people.

It is easy to relate to an inch which is based on the thumb (the French word "pouce" is the same for both). But who can identify with the stuffy centimetre, or the microscopic millimetre — too small to see let alone grasp?

The foot is a human measure, linked firmly to the bottom of your leg. The yard harks back to the stride of a royal king. But what of the metre?

The French Republican government instituted the metre in 1791. They defined it as follows: 1/10,000,000th the length of the earth's meridian running from the North Pole to the Equator — through Paris. Today the metre has been modernized to give it more relevance. Since 1960, it is defined as : "equal in length to 1,650,763.73 wavelengths of the orange-red line in the spectrum of the Krypton-86 atom — under specified conditions."

Imagine the technocrats behind these definitions and it's not surprising that metric language is hard on the ear. The metric system may be more rational than the imperial one — but it is far less poetic.

A miss is good as a kilometre will never have the same ring as a miss is as good as a mile. Jack was every centimetre a sailor would not have caught on as a sea shanty. That great old tune: *I love you a bushel and a peck, a bushel and a peck, I do*, would have turned into: *I love you 35.23808 litres and 0.009092175 cubic metres, I do, 35.23808 litres and 0.009092175 cubic metres I do.*

Hardly the stuff of Grammy awards.

Not surprisingly, the U.S. rebelled against the metric system as soon as it came within a few kilometres. But shortly after Britain converted, Canada obediently followed suit, leaving millions of imperialists stranded — metric illiterates — ignorant of their own height and weight.

Yet I fear worse to come. I can already hear the Bureaucrats of Metrification, rationalizing more changes: Our measure of time is illogical, they will say. There are 60-minute hours, 24-hour days, 7-day weeks and 12 months in a year. Why not make it uniform, and base it all on 10? Re-invent the second: call it a decisec.

Ridiculous, you say?

In the 1790s the leaders of the French Revolution tried to do something similar when they instituted a reform of the calendar. A special national committee of ministers, mathematicians, and scientists devised a new calendar — based on the number 10. There were 100 seconds in every minute and 100 minutes in every hour. There were 10 hours in a day and 10 days in a week — which was called a "decade."

The system was instituted and lasted 13 years, before the public rebelled. Napoleon finally abolished it, restoring the old calendar. Lunacy, you say? Who were the madmen on the committee that devised this crazy calendar?

Exactly the same people who invented the metric system.

BAGUELS 'N' LOX
(THE EMPAÑADA & THE
APOSTROPHE KILLER)

•

•

•

"Office de la Langue Française," said a cool female voice as I gripped the phone ready for battle. I had reached the Quebec department responsible for 'francicizing' English signs.

The apostrophe killers.

I wanted some information — whether or not the word "bagel" was allowed on outside signs — and I expected the cold shoulder. Like many anglos, the language "office" conjured up for me a vision of wire-spectacled bureaucrats roasting English words over an open fire — and the experience hadn't started well. I'd spent two hours getting busy signals, then 25 minutes on hold.

Now I was talking to a government Language Lady who wanted to know the nature of my "linguistic difficulty."

"The bagel," I replied. "Is 'bagel' legal on outside signs?"

"Ah! Le bagel!" she cried with unexpected enthusiasm. "We just had a new ruling on that last week."

She rummaged noisily through some files and returned to the phone with breathless excitement.

"Oui, monsieur! Under the ruling, the word bagel is permissible! It is "a masculine noun derived from the Jewish word *bey-gel*.

"But the 'Office' recommends another spelling," she continued. "The English spelling B-A-G-E-L is pronounced 'bag-elle' in French. To encourage the correct French pronunciation the 'Office' recommends it be spelled: B-A-G-U-E-L."

"Bagwell?" I said.

"Non, monsieur," said the Language Lady. "You must pronounce the 'ue' sound, as it is said in French — *ueu*."

"Baguuuuuhhll" I said, giving it my best Anglo effort.

"Non, monsieur *ueueue*. Ba-*guele!* Many English people have difficulty with this sound. Try again."

"*Ueueue!*" I said tightly. "Ba-*geueueueull!* But how will anyone know what I mean?"

"Oh monsieur," she giggled. "Everyone in Quebec knows the bagel. It is delicious."

The Language Lady advised me that the new ruling was just a recommendation. Montreal's legendary Bagel Factory won't have to sell *baguels* — though the Language Lady would like to see it.

"Try to understand" she explained. "It isn't easy in a world where everything is automatically spelled in English.

"Take Japanese tofu," she said. "The Japanese pronounce it "toe-foo" — and that's how it is spelled in English: T-O-F-U.

"But in French, T-O-F-U comes out of the mouth as 'tofeu.' . . . So we recommend it be spelled T-O-F-O-U in Quebec."

I enquired about other ethnic food pronunciations: the Greek souvlaki (same spelling as English), and the Spanish empañada. But the language lady was puzzled.

"C'est quoi ça, un 'empañada'?" she asked — and I heard her rifling through more reference books.

"Non monsieur, it is not in the Petit Robert Dictionary . . . or in the Time-Life book of exotic foods, or in my Quebec Guide to Writing Menus.

"Let me try Larousse Gastronomique . . . . Et voila! E-M-P-A-Ñ-A-D-A." And she began to read aloud: "*A small crusted pastry or turnover stuffed with minced meat, spices, onions and olives.*"

"That's it!" I said, but she kept on reading, clearly intrigued.

"*Originally from Galicia, it is classically prepared with chicken or fish . . . but can also be served with seafood or sardines.*"

Her accent was exquisite and she rolled her r's, savouring each ingredient like a chef. My mouth watered.

"Mmmmmmmm . . ." sighed the Language Lady. "Did you know, monsieur, that in Chile and Argentina they stuff it with melon, raisins and olives, and add cumin and paprika? They recommend it be served very hot — with red wine . . . Mon dieu! It sounds delicious, non? Where can I try one for lunch?"

I recommended an empañada joint to her, and she filled me in on some more new culinary P's and Q's.

Under "Office" guidelines, a muffin is a *moufflet*, while pretzels are spelled *bretzels* (words few French-Quebecers know). The word *hot-dog* is recommended along with *chien chaud* — but hamburger is heavily frowned upon, in favour of *hambourgeois*.

Barbecue chicken is *poulet à la broche* — not poulet barbecue — but *sauce barbecue* is quite acceptable.

It's hard work finding correct French translations, lamented the Language Lady — especially with an ever-growing list of English words: new food

59

products, computer terms and technical jargon that threaten to sweep over the French language like the waves over King Canute.

So many people called the "Office" with so many questions, she said, that it was difficult to give each enough time. I looked at my watch: the Language Lady had given me 25 minutes of her time to explain the spelling of bagel and empanada. And a very pleasant 25 minutes, at that. I felt a strange fondness for her.

As is often the case in Quebec, I disagreed with much of the message, but I got along fine with the messenger. Despite our language differences, I liked the Language Lady and she liked me. I was tempted to invite her out for an empanada, but didn't push the relationship too fast. In this language-obsessed province, I was sure we would have other opportunities: more outdoor signs to discuss, more pronunciations to debate, more ethnic dishes to share over the phone.

"C'était un plaisir de vous parler, monsieur." said the Language Lady warmly. "Au revoir, monsieur!"

"*Salut*, madame," I said, pursing my lips, as in bay-*gueule*.

"*Uuuuhh*, monsieur," she said. "It is pronounced *saluuuuut*."

And the Language Lady laughed.

HOW THE WORLD WORKS

•

•

•

Recently, I delved into the psychology of people who pay bills on time versus those of us who procrastinate. Yet bills are really a symptom — a tiny skirmish in an unending struggle between the planet's two major groups of people. Not men against women. Not communists versus capitalists. Type M (Messy) versus Type N (Neat).

Which are you?

If you're a Type M (Messy), you're easy to spot. As you read this column, your shirt is sticking out of your pants. Your bedroom looks like burglars have ransacked it. You are always searching for things: addresses, underwear and especially your keys — which are probably in your pocket.

Type N (Neat) is harder to spot — though YOU know exactly who you are. It is written down in the agenda you keep in your breast pocket. You plan your winter holidays every May, and rented a hall for your daughter's wedding the day she was born. You set your watch-alarm to beep one hour before the garbage truck arrives. If you don't pay your bills on time, there is an excellent chance you are dead.

Unlike Type M, you waste no time looking for things, because your whole life is spent organizing them. You are always crossing something off your agenda, updating old lists, creating new ones. There are two pens in your pocket, in case one runs out of ink.

Type M often buys an agenda too, but forgets to use it. Instead, M's purse or pocket is stuffed with bits of paper — so crumpled they can't be read. If M carries a pen, it is usually leaking.

An excellent place to study the difference between M and N is the office. Type M's office looks like it's just been through a terrorist attack: Giant piles of paper litter the floor and all other horizontal surfaces; a billion scraps of paper are tossed randomly about, as if someone had been shredding documents.

Yet as far as M is concerned, EVERY bit of paper is incredibly important. If someone accidentally moves anything, M panics.

"You threw out the styrofoam cup with crumpled subway transfers in it? . . . No! — Not *that!* They were the coupons for my savings bonds."

By comparison, N's office looks like it hasn't been used since N moved in: colour-coded folders, files, pens and envelopes stacked as precisely as in a stationery store; huge Rolodex card files containing every telephone number N has ever dialed.

"You want the Tanzanian trade delegate in Medicine Hat? Don't look it up. I've got it right here."

The home is another good litmus test. M's kitchen looks like a chemistry lab after an explosion. The table is stained the colour of petrified spaghetti sauce; the fridge contains molds advanced enough to create penicillin.

M may own a dishwasher — but only to hide dirty dishes. There are no plates in the cupboard. Before eating, M takes a plate out of the dishwasher and washes it by hand. By contrast, N's cupboards groan with gleaming stacks of dishes. N will wash them again *before* eating on them, in case dust has gathered since they were last done.

And while N's house is clean enough to perform brain surgery on the floor, it is never clean enough.

"It doesn't usually look like this," N immediately advises visitors, "the cleaning woman just had a heart attack."

The most fascinating thing about M and N is that neither can spend much time with their own type. When two Type M's live together their combined mess horrifies them both; worse, they are always fighting over WHOSE mess it is.

"I didn't even eat dinner here last night . . . It's *your* pizza in the bathtub!"

When two Type N's live together, things are clean but tense. Neither one can adjust to the other's system of neatness.

"Why do you put your underwear and socks in the *same* drawer," says one. "It's much easier if you store everything alphabetically."

"That's idiotic," replies the other. "And why do you keep putting beer mugs in with the glasses? They obviously belong with the cups."

Shut off from their own kind, M and N are inevitably forced to marry each other. Secretly, N is convinced that M can be converted, that inside this Messy person is a Neat person dying to get organized.

Nothing could be more wrong. Being messy is a genetic condition — no more changeable than the freckles on your face, or your ability to program a video recorder. In fact, M is marrying N convinced that N will clean up after them forever. This too is wrong.

M and N will spend the rest of their lives arguing over when to do the dishes, who should take out the garbage and who has the keys.

This is called love.

WAITING FOR THE WAITER

.

.

.

Welcome to the "service decade." No — not community service or religious service. Service in restaurants. According to a recent survey by American Express, the 1990s are a time when people want friendlier waiters and "restaurants that embrace."

At last, I may be ahead of my times: I've been in the embrace of restaurants most of my life. Ever since I was old enough to cook I've been eating out, looking for a better meal than I can burn myself. There are restaurants I've eaten in more often than my own kitchen, waiters who know me so well they give my order to the chef before coming to my table.

At La Bodega, a Spanish haunt of mine, my selection is so predictable the waiters always address me as "Monsieur Omelette."

Yet if waiters know me, I also know them. I've shared my dinner with them for years, admiring their skills, cursing their ills, battling their wills. So, as the "service decade" dawns, here is Freed's complete Field Guide to the World of the Waiter and Waitress:

THE PARIS-TRAINED WAITER: Brought up in the trenches of Montmartre, this waiter can walk by you a dozen times and never even see you — although you are a foot away, waving both arms and shouting for a fork, a menu, a meal — along with everyone else in the room.

When he finally decides to visit the table you quickly realize you are too ignorant to eat there. The look on his face tells you that the wine you have ordered is mouthwash and your entrée of melon is supposed to be dessert.

Recently I asked a waiter at a bistro what "Poulet Julienne" was.

"Obviously sir," he said icily. "It is chicken . . . prepared in the style Julienne."

The Paris-trained waiter will not serve you a glass of water, even if you are choking to death on the restaurant floor. He avoids giving you the bill with such determination you would think he was the one who had to pay. The only way to attract his attention is to get up and quietly slip toward the door.

He will get there before you.

THE EXISTENTIALIST: This waiter is not *really* a waiter, He is a writer, or an actor, or a sculptor trapped in the costume of a waiter.

He hates his job, he hates his restaurant and he hates his customers — above all you. Throughout dinner, you feel you are dining on the edge of a razor blade, only a slight move from disaster. If you ask for the salt he is liable to break into tears; send back your meal and he may kill the chef.

When this waiter takes your order, he always writes copious notes — but 75 minutes later he brings you the wrong dish. In fact, he wasn't taking your order at all; he was taking notes for a screenplay he is writing — about a waiter who is really a writer.

THE HOVERER: Found only in over-priced restaurants, this waiter actually pays *too* much attention to you. He is always scurrying about your table, emptying the ashtray and filling the breadbasket. If you lift your water glass he lifts the pitcher; when you take a bite of bread he catches the crumbs.

He makes you so nervous you lose your appetite. Again and again, he asks: "Is everything satisfactory sir . . . Can I be of assistance?"

Especially when your mouth is full.

THE TALKING MENU: A super-friendly waiter found in the U.S. and Ontario, its behaviour varies with the terrain.

— The United States: "Hi folks, I'm Sue . . . I'll be your serving person this evening. Our special of the night is the double-nacho-and-jalapeno-pepper-burger with creamy-Eyetalian-house-dressing-and-avocado-dipped- potato skins.

"You all gimme a shout when you're ready to order. Have a good one!"

— Toronto: "Good evening. My name is Walter and I'll be supervising your table. I'd like to thank you for being with us this evening and advise you of the dishes our staff will be presenting.

"For starters, we have the stone-dried, Indonesian freshwater crab in a light veloute of baby goat milk and Sargasso seawater. It's garnished with fresh musk-melon and sun-dried grape skins that have been hand-peeled by Japanese monks living in silence in a remote village on Mt. Fujiyama."

Between courses he tells you about his skiing chalet in Colorado where he plans to open a vegetarian sushi barbecue house catering only to overweight movie stars. He is so friendly you should really invite him to pull up a chair and join you — but you fear he might accept.

THE WAITRESS FROM HEAVEN: Usually in her mid-fifties she has made restaurant work a form of community service. She balances so many trays on her arm she should be a professional juggler. She never uses a note-pad but remembers your order better than you.

"OK, honey, you're having the double-cheese burger, extra relish, easy on the mayonnaise, half-order bacon, medium-crisp, cole slaw on the side . . . She's having the eggs, over-easy, hold the hash browns, double sausage, rye toast, margarine-not-butter, de-caf coffee, double-cream and saccharine, separate bills. Now what did I forget?"

She effortlessly handles every customer in the room, from the drunken engineering students to the professional "send-it-back-to-the-chef" artist; she divides your $26 meal into 8 bills of $3.24 to save you tax, and wraps up your leftovers as if she was your mother . . .

Part therapist, part cleaning woman, part restaurant manager she reminds you that being a waiter or waitress is one of the toughest, most thankless jobs around. Which is why I still prefer any waiter — the Paris-trained one, the Existentialist, even the Hoverer — to the alternative.

Self-service.

I WIN AGAIN

•

•

•

CONGRATULATIONS . . . YOU HAVE BEEN SPECIALLY SELECTED TO READ THIS COLUMN. DONT MISS THIS UNIQUE OPPORTUNITY TO BECOME RICH RICH RICH . . . READ ON AND WIN FABULOUS PRIZES.

Dear READER:
It's time I took a new approach to my column and encouraged you — my UNIQUE READER — to profit from your good fortune in reading it. So you have been *computer-selected* to read this week's column and have a chance to WIN WIN WIN.

Because YOU are the kind of reader I want.

You see, dear READER, after several weeks away I've noticed a new kind of junk mail piling up on my doorstep. Every second envelope has my name in foot-high type along with rafts of promises. Things like:

> *Congratulations* JOSH FREED *on being selected for an opportunity to win a handsome prize* . . . .
> Win a MILLIONAIRE'S CAR loaded down with a panoply of creature comforts . . . along with a MILLIONAIRE'S BANKROLL . . . SUBSCRIBE NOW TO TRUCKSTOP MAGAZINE.

The trend seemed to start with the advent of computer addresses, though the offers were fairly simple at first. I remember being puzzled when *Encore* magazine sent me a cheque for $10 to be paid if I took something called a "preferred traveller card."

I was flattered when *House & Home* magazine invited "JOSH FREED . . . to enjoy a FREE COPY of the beautiful new guide to decor design and the good life" because I was the "kind of person" they wanted. Not only did they know my name, but they showered it across the page more times than a love poem. And it was just the start.

Fortune magazine offered me a trial subscription. I was the kind of person who should be "MANAGING THE 80s" and discovering "AMERICA'S MOST ADMIRED CORPORATIONS."

I even got a FREE WELLNESS LETTER from the University of California in

Berkeley "to help JOSH FREED maintain your most valuable asset — your wellness." They also offered to help me rank my problems by letting me take a "free Hassle Index Test."

WARNING. DO NOT STOP READING THIS COLUMN. YOU COULD WIN A $10,000 BONUS IF YOU ANSWER THE SKILL-TESTING QUESTION AT THE END. WHY THROW AWAY THE CHANCE TO MAKE A MILLION ?

The pace became feverish, as *Maclean's* magazine began to pursue me. First, I was "selected" to receive a FREE POCKET CLOCK CALCULATOR or a SUPERJACKET. When I resisted the bait they offered me the special FREED ALARM CLOCK (presumably it only works after 11:00 a.m.).

Fortune magazine upped the ante promising me a GIFT PRIZE of an ULTRONIC MICRO RECORDER — if only I knew what that is. And I reached the zenith of my fame when *Time* magazine offered a 4-piece travel set to Mr. Josh Sreed.

"Why does *Time* magazine want Mr. JOSH SREED?" it asked. "Well, to be candid, we believe you are exactly the kind of person *Time* was created to serve, Mr. Sreed."

Yet none of the lures rivalled three envelopes I found on returning to Montreal last week. Dear READER, compare the incredible offers!!

#1

"You could be the supergrand prize winner MR. JOSH FREED in the $250,000 supercontest draw," trumpeted *Maclean's*, repeating my name seven times.

#2

"The FREED HOME . . . has been placed on the list for the LIFETIME SECURITY SWEEPSTAKES OF $550,000." announced *Reader's Digest*. They used my name eight times.

#3

Time magazine had taken remedial spelling and gotten my name right, emblazoning it on an envelope as big as my kitchen table. My heart stopped when I saw the words: JOSH FREED SHALL BE PAID ONE MILLION DOLLARS. Ripping it open I saw what looked like a stock certificate for a million dollars and a promise to "double my million" *if* I entered and won the "Time Double Your Million Sweepstakes" quickly.

My name appeared 20 times. There was also a sticker that looked like a consumer protection notice saying: "FAIR WARNING . . . if you have the winning number and do NOT claim your prize we MUST award it to someone else." It included 2 stickers saying:

YES.   I want to win the prize.

NO.   Give it to someone else.

Time magazine's content was barely hinted at. Like other publishers, they aren't really selling magazines — they're selling lottery tickets, with magazines tossed in as a betting bonus.

Why play Loto-Quebec where the provincial government takes your money for nothing when you can play Loto-Magazine — and get a FREE *Time* or *Maclean's* subscription tossed in. You don't even have to read it.

BONUS BONUS BONUS OFFER.
CONGRATULATIONS again, dear READER . . . . You've just become eligible for one of our UNIQUE SPECIAL bonus grand prizes — if you keep reading this column to the end.
    QUADRUPLE your MILLION. Win a buried MAYAN TREASURE, the EMPIRE STATE BUILDING, all of PRINCE EDWARD ISLAND and MORE.
LUCKY YOU! READ ON!

The recent Time offer is so incredible I can't wait to see what arrives in my mail next. A package that springs a jack-in-the-box showering confetti and gifts on my floor — so I'll order *Bridal Magazine*?

A TAX HOLIDAY in Bermuda, if I order *Accountant's Monthly Journal*?

A NIGHT with ELVIS — if I subscribe to *National Enquirer*?

Maybe I'll be invited to join a private health insurance scheme with a SPECIAL introductory offer:

CONGRATULATIONS. You have been COMPUTER-SELECTED TO WIN A FREE LIVER TRANSPLANT if you buy your policy before July 31. Optional prizes: WIN A HEART, LUNGS, A NEW BRAIN . . . Expiry date, Oct. 31.

Anyway, if I can't lick 'em I may as well join 'em.

SO DON'T FORGET TO KEEP READING THIS COLUMN.
A million dollars COULD be yours if you keep reading.
DON'T STOP READING and let someone else get YOUR million.
DETAILS TO BE REVEALED IN A FUTURE COLUMN . . . .
DONT MISS IT. KEEP READING THIS COLUMN.
EVERY WEEK. *

---

* Winners to be announced before midnight, Fri. Dec. 31, 2090.

Main Life

ROOM
TO LET

רום
צו פארענטען

Apply To_____

The Main, circa 1932

CHAMBRE
À LOUER

The Main, 1990

BICYCLE BOB RIDES AGAIN

.

.

.

The doorbell was ringing insistently; the caller clearly excited.

"Today is the happiest day of my life!" he announced bounding up my stairs. "My heart is full of joy. My karma is great . . . I've achieved a world first. HA!

"I'm leading a bike trip . . . to Vietnam."

The visitor was Bicycle Bob Silverman, an eccentric 54-year-old Montrealer who's been ringing my doorbell for years with news of his exploits.

Silverman is the chief spoke of Citizens on Cycles — a Montreal bicycle rights group that's run a 15-year crusade against the car. Bob has lied down in rush-hour traffic covered in fake blood to protest the "auto-cracy." He has gone to prison for painting illegal bike paths in the dead of night.

He bicycles in the fiercest blizzards; he screams at careless motorists. He knows the number of bikes in Kyoto, bikepaths in Amsterdam, bike parking lots in Copenhagen. He is the Johnny Appleseed of the bicycle world.

This time Silverman had outdone himself. After several months of lobbying, he had convinced the Government of Vietnam to let him lead the first organized bike tour of that country — a two-week odyssey along footpaths and canals long closed to outsiders.

The world's most passionate cyclist was going to the Shangri-la of bicycling; he was so excited he broke into one of his many poems:

> I will bike the streets of Saigon,
> I will walk the lanes of Hue [pronounced *Huay*]
> I will drive the Mekong Delta,
> On a bicycle highway

"Did you know that bikes carried all the supplies for the battle of Dien Diem Phu!" he announced. "They were the jeeps of the Ho Chi Minh Trail!

"It's the only way to see Vietnam . . . There are more bikes than cars; more bikers per capita than anywhere on earth. In Vietnam, WE are the majority. HA!"

To fully appreciate Bob's enthusiasm, you need to have followed the extraordinary career of this committed *velorutionary* (from the French word *velo*, for bike). I first met him in the late 1960s before he became Bicycle Bob. Back then he was known as Volleyball Bob — because he was leading a crusade for municipally-sponsored volleyball courts. Bob is an anarchist, and he felt volleyball suited his politics. He'd written something called "The Volleyball Manifesto" — outlining the ten "ecological and humane principles of volleyball" (ie. It doesn't take much space to play; the equipment is cheap; everyone rotates positions, etc.).

"Volleyball is six hearts that beat as one," said Volleyball Bob.

Most people laughed — but Bob harangued the city's recreation department so persistently that they finally gave him some courts, near Mount Royal. Over 100 nationalities have played there in the last 17 years — from a Samoan gigolo to some Libyan soldiers visiting Montreal. It is undoubtedly the longest-running, self-managed anarchist volleyball game on earth — and Bob is at its heart, still reciting poetry.

> Our jobs are tough, our nights are short,
> So let's be kind on the volleyball court.

Yet no sooner were the nets up than Bob had leapt to a new challenge — the Battle for the Bike.

"Bicycling is cyclotherapy," he declared. "It releases pent-up energy and combats auto-eroticism.

"Freud understood; he was a cyclist! Henry Ford did too — he gave up driving at the end of his life and switched to a bike."

When Citizens on Cycles was founded, Montreal had no bike paths and no plans to build them — until city officials met Bob. His demonstrations, protests and "die-ins" were soon all over the news. He dressed up as Moses, and tried to "part" the St. Lawrence River, to underline the need for a bridge for bikes. Eventually, he got it.

He stormed the Metro with other cyclists, to win the right to bring bikes on board. He organized an International Bicycle Day that is now celebrated in 14 countries — from Australia to Japan.

People mocked Bob, but today there are several hundred kilometres of bike path on the island of Montreal largely because of him. Yet even as Bicycle Bob was winning the war against cars, he was already acquiring a new identity — Visionary Bob.

He had always worn coke-bottle glasses. But several years ago Bob discovered an unusual program that claims to improve bad eyesight through mental and physical exercise. (It was popularized by Aldous Huxley, in the book *The Art of Seeing*.)

Bob was quickly swept up. He started wearing bizarre glasses with black checkered lenses. He organized "eyeclasses" and gave "eyexercises." He repeated the words: *There is nothing wrong with my eyesight*, ten times each morning.

Enthusiasts loved him, optometrists thought he was crazy. But today, Bob has shed his glasses entirely and navigates around town on his own eyepower. I sometimes worry about Bob when I see him squinting as he drives through Montreal's ferocious traffic — but his optometrist assures me Bob's vision is much improved.

With success visible, it was obviously time for a new cause — so Bob decided to return to square one. Because long before he was Volleyball Bob, he was known as Vietnam Bob.

Throughout the sixties, Bob owned a left-wing bookshop and worked for the Quebec Committee Against the War in Indo-China. "I cried during the Christmas bombing . . . I felt it was my own flesh burning." When Vietnam won the war, Bob moved onto Volleyball, then the Velorution, and finally Vision — but Vietnam continued to haunt him.

Two years ago, he started dreaming about visiting that country; and when Bob starts dreaming — look out. He pored over Vietnamese history books. He developed a passion for Vietnamese food. He listened to Vietnamese music, subscribed to Vietnam's newspaper and studied their language, using a "Bulgarian method of super-learning."

"*Toi-muon Vietnam*," chuckles Bob, in his new language. "That means — I love Vietnam."

Bob even went to a Vietnamese summer camp for a week — the only Caucasian in the group — and spent his nights singing Vietnamese folksongs by the campfire. Gangs of children were soon trailing after this strange pied piper, shouting: "*Bob Say-dap! Bob Say-dap!*" — Bicycle Bob, in Vietnamese.

Last year, Bob visited Vietnam for six weeks, by bike of course, and came back exultant.

"Vietnam inspires me. Her people. Her land. Her children. Her struggle against impossible odds," he enthused upon his return. "Her poetry fills my ears with music and my heart with love."

He decided to organize a western bike trip — then applied his considerable powers of persuasion to the reluctant Vietnamese government. After a year of calls and letters from Bob, the Vietnamese government surrendered and gave him a contract to run that country's first international bike tour. He recently led a two-week tour through the Mekong Delta, visiting towns unseen by foreigners since the U.S. army left.

"And we saw it all from the vantage point of the average Vietnamese," says Bob, "on top of a bicycle. HA!"

Yet Bob already has another dream: he wants to move to Vietnam.

"I feel out of place in the consumerism of North America — the cars, the clothes, the money. Everything I do is laughed at here, ridiculed — even though it's always a success.

"In Vietnam they value bikes more than cars, and poets more than businessmen. It's strange . . . but I feel more at home there."

Single, Bob dreams of marriage — to a Vietnamese woman. "There are over a million widows there," he muses, "and anything is possible . . . Actually, I've never liked doing anything but the impossible. The possible has always bored me."

May-man Vietnam. Good luck Vietnam. *Say-dap Bob* may be coming to stay.

In the past year Bicycle Bob has led two bike trips to Vietnam, stopping to play volleyball along the way. He also says he received his "Ph.V." (Doctor of Vision). He is leaving shortly to set up the first "eyeclasses" in Nha Trang, Vietnam.

BARE FEET IN THE PARK

•

•

•

When was the last time 1000 strangers showed up in your front yard chanting political slogans, juggling swords and skulking in the bushes in combat training for WW III ?

All of them will be in my yard for the next few months, as spring rites begin at Mount Royal, the largest park in Montreal, right across the street from my house.

I never know who's coming to visit.

Take the army of high school buglers who appeared a couple of years ago for the International Drum and Bugle Competition. More than 500 freshly-scrubbed faces showed up: their 500 tubas, trumpets and bugles pointed directly at my bedroom window, every morning, for a week — at 7:00 a.m.

The first day I signed a neighbour's petition; the rest of the week I slept at a friend's.

There is also a "demonstration-of-the-month" that starts or finishes in front of my house — usually led by a zealot shouting into a megaphone. For instance, 10,000 angry separatists sang "Gens du Pays" 50 yards from my balcony to protest the signing of the constitution. And thousands of cyclists gathered, led by the piercing battle cry of Bicycle Bob Silverman: "CYCLISTS OF THE WORLD UNITE. YOU HAVE NOTHING TO LOSE BUT YOUR CHAINS."

A festival of Marxist groups waved red banners and sang parts of the Albanian national anthem, a Green protest sang odes to "Mother Earth," and a Spiritual fair featured everything from chanting Hare Krishnas to a 12-hour-long "Cosmic Hum."

Other visitors come alone. There is an elderly Oriental man who arrives at dawn to practise martial arts, kicking his feet in slow motion and crying out in Chinese. And a long-haired young man, whose wheelchair is strapped to a huge pit bull. He gallops down the street at breakneck speed, like a harness racer, terrifying old ladies and motorists.

My favourite park guest is the Great Antonio's landlady: an elderly Eastern European woman who tells me tales of her legendary tenant. Antonio is a 400-pound mountain of man who likes to pull city buses through downtown Montreal, by a chain.

Antonio has never pulled a bus through my park, but his landlady comes there regularly and fills me in on the problems of life with "the world's strongest man."

"A nice boy," she told me last spring, in a thick accent, "but so BIG. Every time he sits on toilet — BOOM — toilet breaks! . . . My son fixes and fixes, but always the same — BOOM — toilet breaks again."

This year she informs me that a new deluxe toilet has been installed and is holding up well — but there is a new problem.

"Such a nice boy, but always at home alone," she says, eyeing me hopefully. "Tell me, do you know any big girls?"

My park is also a training ground for aspiring street entertainers honing their skills for Old Montreal. Recently, a thin young man strung a tightrope between two trees and tottered back and forth on it, until his girl-friend tossed him two juggling pins.

He fell off.

Last year there was a steady parade of clowns and acrobats, including a sword-juggler who kept cutting himself. I think that's why he practises at my park: it's close to the Royal Victoria Hospital.

Just down the block from my house is an armoury: training quarters for the Canadian Grenadier Guards, who use the park for calisthenics. The soldiers regularly jog by my house in formation shouting "HUT! HUT!"; occasionally, they go on late night manoeuvres dressed in camouflage gear.

Disguised as trees, they slither through the moonlit grass, clutching bayonets and scaring passers-by who think the Russians have landed. Still, they are strapping young men who come in handy when my car is stuck in winter.

Oh yes, there is also the noise. On holidays the Africans and Latinos invade the park for life and death soccer rivalries, cheering on their favourite teams in deafening waves of sound that make reading difficult.

On weekends, Molson Stadium is so close by that I can hear the announcer's play-by-play — even with cotton balls stuffed in my ears.

"SECOND DOWN AND TWENTY TO GO . . ."

And every summer Sunday, hundreds of leftover hippies gather for a strange 1960s-style festival: The women dance in bare feet, the men pound on drums so loudly you can hear them in Ottawa.

Despite the racket I get by. I can live with the Marxists and the military, tolerate the buglers and the singing separatists, put up with the occasional flame-thrower, threatening to burn down the park.

But there is one visitor I cannot bear: the park vandal who swoops down from the mountain at night. Most of the time he dismantles swings and see-saws — but when there is nothing else left, he dismantles my car.

In recent years I have lost two mirrors, three hubcaps and a chunk of my rear bumper. Several months ago he pried open the trunk of my car with a crowbar.

So this season I'm taking precautions to protect myself against my parade of uninvited guests. Since spring started, I've been parking my car at my parents' house, doing my reading at the office and spending most nights over at a friend's — and ever since, I find the park is a great place to call home.

As long as I don't have to live there.

THE MAYOR OF THE MAIN

•

•

•

Late afternoon on the Main and the Mayor is in. His office is a city bench in front of Warshaw's supermarket, on St. Laurent boulevard. You can find the Mayor there every afternoon: 3:00–7:00 p.m. Office hours.

He's a big guy, hard to miss. Weighs maybe 300 pounds, wears a battered suede cowboy hat, carries a cane. Knows everyone.

"A landmark . . . I'm a landmark," he says, cigar swirling in his mouth like part of his tongue. "I'm part information booth, part tourist attraction, part history. I been here 64 years . . . 65 come September 11.

"The city oughta pay me to sit here . . . *Whaddya think? Whaddya think?*"

The Mayor's probably got a name, but no one uses it. Friends call him Racko, Tully, or Speck — but to most people he's the Mayor: the Mayor of the Main. He was born just down the block, upstairs of Rossy's department store; now he lives in a small apartment two blocks away.

"I been to Vegas, L.A., Hialeah — here there and everywhere. I made a lotta money. And spent a lotta money — $200,000 in nine years. But I always come back to the Main. Who wants to live in a suburb — gotta drive 20 miles for a rye bread? This is my strip."

For most of his life the Mayor drove a cab in Montreal — though it was "just a sideline." Everything was a sideline, if you ask him.

"I worked as a doorman too. Crap games, blind pigs, strip joints — you name it . . . Worked at the Café Paris too, when Montreal was wide-open.

"What a place! 50 dancing girls and 85 hookers. 85! . . . All of 'em beautiful. Drove a limo too. Liberace paid me 1200 bucks for ten days. I drove Jimmy Durante and Sammy Davis. It was just a sideline mind you. Just a sideline."

Thirteen years ago the Mayor's checkered career ended abruptly when he was crossing Park avenue and got hit by a car.

"Some greaseball kid comes flying through the intersection and knocks me flat. They rushed me to hospital — when I got out I was walking with a cane."

He shrugs his huge shoulders, puffs his cigar.

"I couldn't do much after that . . . Slowed me down . . . Time to retire."

Today the Mayor gets a small military pension, for serving in WW II, stationed in Westmount. It leaves him free to hang around the Main, trying to make a few bucks "on the side." He's usually got something to sell — cheap watches, lighters, jewellery — discretely tucked into a paper bag under the bench, in case a city inspector comes by.

"Watches are a good seller — buy 'em by the box and sell 'em at five bucks a crack. Other times it's wallets, transistor radios, other gimmicks. Whatever I can grab wholesale . . . Anything to make a few bucks.

"Two years ago there was a shortage of safes during New Year's — because of the AIDS scare . . . Someone in the States got me a gross, and I made a few dollars. Whaddya think?"

At the St. Laurent boulevard street fair the Mayor had another operation going. A local kid packaged up some "floral scent" seeds in small plastic bags and the Mayor and him set up shop on a picnic table outside The Main deli.

Long lasting fragrance. Put spring in your drawer said the sign. Beside it, the Mayor, as wide as the table, puffing a cigar and sweet-talking the crowds of passers-by.

"Mesdames et messieurs. Take home something *beautiful*. Fresh from Paris — the bargain of the week. One for five bucks, two for seven bucks.

"Put a little beauty in your home."

The Mayor's not the only one trying to make a buck on the Main. A lot of other characters have been there for decades too. The Mayor knows them all. Like Foster — an old guy, wears a flat cap and walks real slow. Used to be a furrier, no one knows how far back. Maybe 100 years. Today, he works the Main, carrying white plastic bags filled with stuff he gets wholesale. He specializes in three items: cheap socks, underwear and karnatzel sausages.

"Funny combination," says the Mayor, with a shrug. "Socks and sausages. You figure it out."

Then there's The Greek, another Main regular. Usually got twenty watches — right up his arm, just like in the movies.

There's an old guy who collects bits of scrap of metal off the sidewalk to sell by the pound; and a woman who cleans out the garbage pails for bottles and cans — every hour on the hour — like she worked for the city.

"Times are getting hard," says the Mayor. "Everyone's trying to make a buck. A couple of weeks ago, I saw someone scrape orange rinds outa the garbage and suck them clean.

"I ain't seen that since the depression. *Whaddya think?*"

There are other Main regulars, less industrious. Like Crazy Dave — tall guy who's been going up and down the street for 25 years, talking to himself.

"He's a bit off," says the Mayor, twirling a finger around his temple. "He needs a head-job if you know what I mean."

And Big Animal, who comes down to eat smoked meat almost every day — "eats to live and lives to eat."

"There used to be others too — like the Bag Lady and Radio. We called him that cause he was always yapping — like a radio. But they died or disappeared . . . . There's less of us here all the time."

As he talks, people keep coming to pay their respects: local waiters, waitresses, store-owners — waving hello or punching him in the arm gently, saying: *"How ya doing chief?" "Nice to see ya Mayor."*

Even passing tourists approach him, ignoring the dusty suit and the old cowboy hat, to ask instructions to a street or a store. The Mayor gives them all advice.

A bus stops nearby and a guy steps out, spots the Mayor and rushes up to him shouting:

"Tully! Tully! — the best cab driver in Montreal — I haven't seen you in 35 years!"

The guy is in from Washington D.C. — hasn't been back to Montreal in 30 years — and the Mayor's the first face he recognizes. His wife is already tugging at his arm, eager to leave, but the guy is into nostalgia.

"Remember me Tully? I was a friend of Chicky's. Chicky Segal. Remember?"

"Sure, sure," says the Mayor. "I still see Chicky sometimes. I'll give him your regards."

The guy is ecstatic. As he follows his wife away, the Mayor shrugs and says:

"I never seen the guy in my life . . . . Happens all the time. People come up to me — with pot bellies, bald heads, no teeth — and say 'remember me? Remember me from 40 years ago?'

"How can I remember? What do I look like — an elephant?"

The Mayor leans back, adjusts his cowboy hat ("$200 in Houston. Real suede . . . feel it. Go on."). He puffs at his cigar.

"I made a lotta bucks, spent a lot too. But *I* ran money, money never ran me. I never wanted to be a millionaire, I just wanted to live like one."

He finishes his cigar, butts it out, lights another.

"The way I see it now, all you need in life is 25 bucks in your pocket when you wake up in the morning. Then you're okay.

"That's why I'm always selling gimmicks. Hustle, bustle, buy and sell. But I don't only do it for the money. To tell you the truth, it gives me something to do — sit here, talk to people, shoot the breeze. If I make a few bucks that's even better.

"Tomorrow, I got a good connection on clock-radios. Whaddya think? A good seller, eh?

"If you're interested, lemme know in the afternoon . . . Office hours. You know where I'll be."

HOW THE MAYOR GOT ELECTED

Lunchtime on St. Laurent boulevard a couple of months back, and I'm chatting with the Mayor of the Main, a talking history of life on that street.

He was born on the Main, "when Warshaw's was just a hole in the ground" and still lives just up the block.

"My brother was killed right here on St. Urbain street . . . . I still remember the date — Jan. 7, 1930 — I came home for lunch and we had bananas and cream out of the icebox . . . We didn't have fridges back then.

"A few hours later I got the call from the police saying my brother'd been hit by a car . . . Bananas and cream for lunch, I still remember."

On this day the Mayor looks under the weather — dead broke, and wondering where his next meal is coming from. I'm considering buying him lunch, when a voice booms through the cool air:

"Hey, Mr. Mayor! What're you wearing there — a costume? Get a proper tie."

The guy should talk. He's pushing 60, wearing a grey mobster suit — very expensive — with a gold watch on a chain. Working a toothpick around his mouth like a cigar.

"Chubby," shouts the Mayor. "I ain't seen you in years."

"How's my man?" says the newcomer. "Looks like you lost some weight, eh?"

"The Mayor pulls in his immense belly. "Yeah, I took off maybe 50 pounds: lift some weights, a little dieting, a little nookie now and then — strictly for the exercise you know. Cleans out the system."

It turns out Chubby runs a trucking business in the Southern U.S. — he's got a suntan that's hard on the eyes. Back in the 1940s he owned a huge fleet of taxis in Montreal. The Mayor drove one.

"I ran 190 cabs," says Chubby, "and the Mayor was my main driver — the king! You shoulda seen him back then . . . He wore a white sharkskin suit, white shoes and white sox. He had every angle covered.

"All the other drivers would pick up their cars in the morning — not the Mayor. He told me: you want me to drive, I don't come to the car — the car *comes to me* . . . I'd send a cab round to pick him up every day."

The two guys start shmoozing, recalling the Main before the arrival of yuppie clothing shops and chic bistros. "Remember Rabasco's deli — 6 cents and they'd give you a smoked meat sandwich as big as your head," says the Mayor. "And Horseshoe Harry's Place?"

"Schwartz's was just a little joint. Today he's a big shot. Back then he was dying . . . dying. I can remember every building."

With memories flying, I ask about the Mayor's moniker. Why is he known as the Mayor of the Main?

"Now that's a story," says Chubby, and shifting his toothpick in his mouth, he reaches back in his memory for a piece of Montreal folklore you won't find in the history books.

"It all started with Chickie — Chickie Segal — he was a comedian who played the cabarets in the 1940s. Back then, there wasn't much to do in winter — there was no TV or nothing — so Chickie had this idea: run a contest for Mayor of the Main.

"Everyone on the street got involved. We put posters up all over the street, we nominated local characters as candidates, we held meetings where they made fancy speeches.

"Then we rented a hall and the showgirls came down from the cabarets for a real bash, where everyone voted for the Mayor of the street. It became a yearly event . . . We even got Mayor Drapeau to come down one year to award our Mayor the key to the street.

"Fat Label — he weighed almost 500 pounds — he was the Mayor for years. Then he died and the job went to Willie Shortbutt Brown — we called him that because he was always bending down to pick up butts.

"Eventually the title fell to the Mayor here. He'd retired from the cab business, the Main was his turf . . . and the street needed a mayor. It had become a tradition. Peel Street had a mayor then too — Kid Oblay was his name — but I don't know what happened to him."

"He's still around," says the Mayor of the Main. "I went down to Peel to see him a while back. The Kid is maybe 87 now — still hustling and bustling — you know how it is — but he's not looking so good. He had a five o'clock shadow, and didn't even have a deuce on him.

"I took him out for lunch and told him:

'If you're gonna parade around St. Catherine street, you gotta have a shave, Kid. You can't look like crap. Be a *mensch*.' "

The Mayor and Chubby shoot the breeze some more, throwing around more names that sound like they come from a Damon Runyan novel. Before he goes, Chubby's hand flashes out to slip the Mayor something:

A hundred dollar bill.

"Take care of yourself, my man — get a proper tie," says Chubby, heading off. The Mayor pockets the bill swiftly, like a bear swatting its prey.

"Whaddya say?" he says to me. "What timing! I really needed some cash about now and here it is — An act of God . . . . An act of God, I tell ya."

The Mayor sucks in his belly and pulls out a fat, cheap cigar, lighting up. The world is definitely looking better, and so is he.

"Hey, Josh," says the Mayor of the Main. "Whaddya say we go for a steak — at Moishes. Lunch is on me."

STREET MEDICINE

•

•

•

Most people think "bug season" ends in August — but the real Montreal bug season starts in winter, and most people have caught the same "bug" as me. My throat is sore, my nose is blocked and I make snuffling sounds like a wild boar rooting for truffles.

It's the common Canadian cold: the price we pay for living in this country, and the reason we're so keen on medicare. We know we will spend much of our lives sick. If you haven't got a cold you've probably got some kind of flu: the Hong Kong Flu, the Bangkok Flu or the Lac St. Jean–Lake Titicaca exchange program Flu. Last year I had the California Flu, a mellow bug that liked to be fed avocado dip and listen to New Age music.

I'd visit a doctor but he'd just poke me with cold steel objects and say authoritatively: "Well, it looks like you've caught a bug." If it was Black Plague or Polio he'd have just the treatment, but a cold is beyond science's grasp. There is no official cure. That's why most people have their own secret remedy — some ancient tribal remedy handed down from their grandmother that "always works."

In recent days I've been told to take massive doses of Vitamin C, small doses of Vitamin E, B and D; to suck on zinc tablets and boil ginger ale "until there are no more bubbles."

A Hungarian friend recommended inhaling the vapours from Chamomile tea, while a vegetarian advised I ingest raw millet and yogurt. A French film editor with whom I work has forced me to drink large quantities of boiled water and lemon. Other suggested remedies:

MARIO, *my hip Guyanese depanneur owner:*
"Hey man! . . . What you need is the Guyana cure. You take a large glass of very strong white rum, you mix in two limes, two teaspoons of salt and drink it all in one gulp, . . . I guarantee you'll be okay in a few hours."

Mario says Canadians get more colds than Guyanans because most of us don't wear a hat. "The most important thing is to keep your head dry, man . . . You get your head wet for 30 seconds — that's it — you got a cold. Look at me, man . . . I never let my head get wet and if I sneeze once I drink a glass of Guyana potion. I haven't been sick in ten years."

PAUL, *my soft-spoken Italian barber:*
"You take a nice a-red wine . . . You put two parts wine in a nice big pot and boil down to one part. Then you add something very sweet — honey she's good but maple syrup she's not bad too. You drink two glasses and even if you no get better you definitely *feel* better."

"Why do we catch colds?" I asked Paul.

"It's no hard to explain," he said confidently. "It's because you go from a cold place to a warm place or the other way around.

"It's like wine, my friend. You put wine in the cellar in winter and in spring she starts to ferment . . . It's the same with the blood — it ferments or something — I don't know exactly . . .

"But *definitely!* . . . You go from cold to hot — you're dead!"

Paul's theory has much support.

EVELYN, *an old acquaintance, recalls childhood life with her Polish grandmother:*
"Every time we came in during winter she'd make us wait in the vestibule for ten minutes in all our clothing — until she was satisfied our body temperatures had risen to the same temperature as the house.

"It was ridiculous — but she was an old lady so we had to humour her . . . . To tell you the truth we never got any colds."

Finally, over at *Simcha's* Fruit store on The Main, the spry grey-haired couple who run the place insisted I to go home and try a remedy from the "old country" — the Romanian alco-rub.

"Before you go to bed tonight, you must take a very hot shower," explained "Mrs. Simcha" with the precise instructions of a pharmacist.

"Then you rub your whole body in alcohol from head to foot, cover yourself in very thick blankets and put on a *wool hat*. You sweat all night and in the morning that's it — you're cured!"

"We should know," adds Mr. Simcha. "Every time a customer opens the front door we get a draft — so we get colds all the time. Trust me, the alco-rub is the only cure."

Now clearly, as a native-born Canadian, I know all of these remedies are just old wives' tales. There is no magic cure for a bug; my *Encyclopaedia Britannica* flatly states: "There is no specific treatment for the common cold."

But just in case, I am wrapped in blankets and a wool hat, sucking on a zinc tablet with hot ginger ale, and I think I feel a little better. Feel free to help. What is your secret cure? Do you baste your sick spouse in soy sauce and then leave them to hang on the clothesline? Leap in a vat of ice water covered in Preparation H? Or something more traditional: *Eye of newt and toe of frog, wool of bat and tongue of dog?* If you have a secret remedy, please let me know. But for the moment, I'd better go. My wine is boiling.

LITTLE SHOP OF SCHNORERS

.

.

.

It has survived more marriages than Elizabeth Taylor, more bankruptcies than Nelson Skalbania. It's been through the pain of abandonment and the terror of armed robbery; been vandalized by criminals and victimized by law.

Punks, hippies, ethnics and artists have come to it with hope and left with shattered dreams. They say it is cursed — but a new suitor has just arrived, eager to test his luck. It is my corner store, on Duluth Street and Esplanade Avenue: the scene of more dramas than many theatres.

When I first moved into my neighbourhood ten years ago, the shop was easy to miss: a tiny storefront with peeling doors and cracked windows. For most of the century, it had been a grocery, run by an elderly Jewish woman who swept the store and sidewalk each day at dawn. But the woman had died and the store had fallen on hard times, rented out like a cheap hooker to whomever would have it. On my arrival it had just been renovated and re-opened as a depanneur, by a cheerful East-Indian who left the door wide open, until he ran into an ugly slice of Montreal life.

Vandals threw rocks through his windows. Thieves smashed in the door and stole crates of beer. He was held up at knifepoint and by gun, getting more paranoid with each attack. By the end of his second year, I had to knock to get into the store for a quart of milk. Eventually, the vandals were caught: rich teenagers from a fashionable district, out for kicks. But it was too late. My once-cheerful depanneur owner had quit in dismay, leaving the store abandoned and bare.

A desolate winter passed. With spring came new occupants: a bubbly young waitress and her boyfriend, filled with fresh dreams. The waitress had diligently saved her tips for several years. She wanted to convert the tiny hole-in-the-wall into a "gourmet grocery": a "food boutique" with classy hand-made shelves.

All spring they painted and pampered the little shop — and somehow the shelves became an obsession. For weeks, the boyfriend chopped lumber, constructing a Great Wall of Shelving in the tiny space; for months more, he bevelled and sanded, varnished and stained.

"When will it be finished?" asked passers-by, admiring the Great Wall. "Soon!" he would say, continuing to sand, as his girlfriend forked out another month's rent.

By mid-summer the shelves were still unfinished, and the waitress' money was gone. There were quarrels, threats — the boyfriend vanished — but the waitress refused to give up. There was no money for expensive groceries, so she sold ice cream cones until fall came and sales plunged. She tried making sandwiches — but the city said she needed a restaurant permit and ordered her to stop. Her dreams dashed, the waitress suffered a nervous breakdown, and the store went broke. I bought a section of the Great Wall — for $25.

Another bleak winter, another spring redolent with fresh paint. White paint. Pastel-coloured lamps. Long, clean tables and nifty metal shelves that were sort of . . . post-industrial chic.

My little store was a graphic arts studio.

The owners were two young women: a lively duo who waved at everyone who passed. They looked busy, happy, successful; my store glowed with new health. The whole neighbourhood was impressed, including the landlord, who doubled the rent. The women fled to cheaper quarters, stripping the store bare.

A year passed. The landlord failed to get his inflated rent, the vacant store paying for his greed. Snow and sleet peeled away the paint, the windows cracked. The building was sold, the rent reduced and the dream factory was open again.

The cheery white walls were painted bilious green, laced with swirls of rat-grey and mud-brown. The shop was furnished in witches' black, a claustrophobe's nightmare, cheerful as a coffin. It was a "new wave" fashion store, selling asymmetrical dresses and off-centre jackets, t-shirts with holes, hats with remarkable shapes. It was clothing for extra-terrestrials — though none lived on our block.

The store was bereft of customers, and those who entered were quick to leave. Each day, we anticipated its closing, yet somehow it stayed open, defying the laws of bankruptcy for two years. What was their secret? Rumours swirled: The owners designed clothing for rock stars. They outfitted theatre companies. They worked for Hollywood. A black Mercedes occasionally stopped to pick up packages: drug-crazed rock stars, placing their order by telephone?

We never found out. Early this year, the fashion store moved out as mysteriously as it had arrived. My store was alone again, as if the very ground beneath it was cursed. Could no one survive?

June, and the familiar smell of paint, and dreams. Inside the shop: a tall

young man, hard at work painting over the bleak walls and assembling —
a Great Wall of shelves!

Aghast, I warned him of the former occupants' fatal obsession, but he only
laughed. The shelves were ready-made, he assured me, and would be up in
days. He was opening an English-language bookstore, a difficult challenge
in French-speaking Montreal.

My neighbours were sceptical. It's an out-of-the-way location for a
bookstore, said one. It'll never work, said another. The *curse*.

When the new store, *Ficciones*, opened, it surprised us all. The latest
version of the Great Wall is packed with books: a terrific selection of prose
and poetry. The place is busier than I've seen it in years, far exceeding the
new owner's modest expectations.

Ahead lies the bleak winter that has broken others, but the young man is
blinded by romance. He plans poetry readings, literary gatherings, a busier
social calendar than my tiny shop has ever known. The young man likes my
store, and it seems my store likes him.

After a decade of failures, carpetbaggers and passers-through, the little
shop on my street is ready for a long-term relationship: someone to replace
the elderly Jewish woman who tended it faithfully for 40 years. I think the
latest suitor may last. But even if he goes broke, all is not lost. I can always
use some extra shelves.

*Two years after this was written, Ficciones is still prospering. My store has never
looked better.*

My Life (Born Freed)

JUST JOSHING

•
•
•

There I was sprawled on a beach in Maine minding my own business when a voice boomed out from behind me:

"Stop that, Josh . . . Do you hear me, Josh?! . . . Jo-o-ssh!!

"JAW-AW-AWWWWWSSSSHHHHH!!"

Like a guilty schoolkid, I dropped the book I was reading and leapt up to face my accuser — but she was turned the other way, bawling out a four-year-old trying to set fire to a cocker spaniel. He was the Josh in question, and I was caught in the crossfire — the third time that afternoon I'd been yelled at by a parent angry at "Josh."

An infuriated father had ordered me to stop punching my sister, mothers had told me to stop wiping my nose with my hand and to put my bathing suit back on *immediately.*

I leapt at every command with a long-conditioned reflex, a response I may have to change. After a lifetime of obscurity my name has been discovered: ripped from the arcane pages of the Bible and flung onto the front lines of the birth announcement pages, along with Jason, Jennifer and Jessica. Suddenly, every Tom, Dick and Harry is named Josh.

What happened?

I grew up in an era where boys had snappy all-American names like Tom, Bill, John and Mike. Girls had cutesy names like Susie, Sally or Sandy. Biblical names like mine were very square, suggesting a greenhorn just off the boat.

Jason and Matthew quickly became Jay and Matt. Joshua became Josh. It could have been worse. Some kids had been named after relatives with old-fashioned names like Gertrude, Edwina, Horace and Delbert. I'd even read of kids whose parents had named them after Marx, Stalin, De Gaulle and Caesar; another who'd been named after a fried fruit dish called Klafouti.

In France, they actually have a law to prevent parents from giving their kids "ridiculous names." Among names they have vetoed are Manhattan, Cherry and Prune.

I was named after my grandfather, Joshua — a good solid name in its day, in Russia — but good for little but ridicule in my own time. In high school,

I was known as a kid with a "weird name"; I spent much of my childhood repeating my name and spelling it.

"Not G-o-s-h, you turkey . . . J-o-s-h!"

Twerps with names like Jeff, Doug and Dan teased me with witty one-liners like "You're joshing me . . . haw haw haw." Or sang "Joshua Fought the Battle of Jericho" for the 11th time that afternoon. Others couldn't pronounce my name. Spanish-speaking kids called me Hosh, East-Indians made it sound like Ghosh, Portuguese used Jorge or even Jesus. To francophones I was inevitably Jacques — until the 1980s when I finally found a similar-sounding word they could understand.

"Josh." I would say to them. "Comme votre raquette de *squash*."

When I reached bill-paying age there were new names on every envelope. The City of Montreal called me Jean. Hydro addressed me as Gosh Fred . . . until I complained. Ever since, it's been Georges.

No one got a bigger kick out of all this than my Uncle Harry. While I was the only Josh on the block, Harry's name was as common as every Tom and Dick's.

"When I was a kid," says Harry, "people were always talking about Harry — Harry Macmillan and Harry Truman, Oil Can Harry, Harry's Bar and Harry Houdini.

"I heard my name so often that eventually I assumed they were never talking about me . . . People would shout 'Look out Harry!' and I wouldn't even turn around. I knew they meant someone else."

But as the old saw goes: "everything that goes around comes around," and in the 1980s, the Bible struck back. As atheism rose, so did the desire to name kids after Biblical characters. People who didn't know Cain from Abel were suddenly hunched over the Good Book debating the sound of Noah and Samuel, Rachel, Sarah, Rebecca, Moses and Matthew.

Lifetime atheists were scouring obscure passages in the Old Testament for names that hadn't yet been discovered: Lemuel? Esau? Lot?

Parental negotiations can be intensive.

HER: I know Magic Johnson is your favourite basketball player, dear — but what kind of name is Magic for a child? . . . How about something more classical, biblical — like Nebudchadnezzar?
HIM: No good. They'll end up calling him Neb.

With the Bible hunt in full gear it was only a matter of time before they stumbled on Joshua. In 1985, Josh was already a rising star. By 1986 it was listed in the top 25 North American names, by 1987 the top 15. This year I am convinced it is entering the top five, eclipsing other popular J-names like Jason, Jessica and Jesse.

Lately my name keeps showing up in newspaper articles about kids —
with headlines like "Dressing little Josh to look Posh."

Recently, a Boston *Globe* editorial put down the generation of yuppie
kids born with Reeboks on their feet and birthmarks shaped like alligators.
Scornfully, it referred to them as "every little Jennifer and Josh."

What next?

A president named Josh? Little Josh and Jessica dolls? A movie called Meet
Josh Doe?

As for my Uncle Harry, he's been pretty much forgotten in recent years.
His name is passé — an off-the-boat greenhorn name that few self-respect-
ing yuppies would give to their Airedale, let alone their kid.

"The trouble with Harry," says Harry, "is that it's become too distinctive.
When people say Harry nowadays, I know they mean me — only me.
There's no getting away from it.

"I feel like a criminal who's been fingerprinted . . . Sometimes I miss the
old days when I was just another name in the crowd — just another Jason,
Justine or Josh."

MY LEFT ARM

.
.
.

You've probably heard of *My Left Foot*, the inspiring, true-life story of a severely handicapped man who learned to paint and write with his foot. Well, in recent weeks, I too have learned to use a hapless piece of my anatomy I'd long overlooked — until a recent injury forced me to rely on it.

My left arm.

My tiny ordeal began during a recent ball hockey game, when I was tripped, and crashed to the pavement heavily like a freshly-cut tree. My last recollection is a voice saying: "Well, I guess he's got his column for next week."

My next one is the ceiling of the Royal Victoria Hospital, whizzing by as an orderly wheeled me in for x-rays on a mobile bed.

A doctor explained that I had "separated" my shoulder and would be sidelined for several weeks. "But look at the bright side," added the cheerful x-ray woman: "At least you've got a column for next week."

I arrived home with my right arm in a sling and strict orders to avoid using it. As if I had a choice. Removed from the sling, it dropped to my side like the sleeve of an empty jacket.

It took only a few hours without my right arm to come to a terrible realisation — my left limb is utterly useless, a free-loader that's been living off my right arm for most of its life. Sure, it can grip a can of tuna while my right hand opens it, or keep a nail steady while my right arm hammers it — but my left arm can't do anything for itself.

It can't slice bread, it can't peel an orange and it can't twirl pasta. It can barely get a fork into my mouth without hitting my cheek. It is an extra appendage — an emergency arm — there like a spare tire. And not even a good one.

Brushing my teeth has become an exhausting ordeal, because my left hand grips a toothbrush like a lobster using chopsticks. Flossing is next to impossible with one hand: I need a second person with a separated shoulder to help out.

My left arm simply cannot cut the mustard; it can't even spread it. Take my writing. Normally, I am an agile one-finger "hunt and peck" typist, capable of some 40 words a minute, with my right index finger. But my left hand is so dim-witted it can't reach half the letters on the keyboard; it makes so many spelling mistakes I look illiterate.

Befoxe ag f9iend helped rerype this par/3*aph, ix looced rike this, becausx ig waz typid by mg beft zand.

Like any creature that cannot manage its own life, my left arm attracts much pity. Senior citizens open office building doors for me; cashiers re-pack my groceries in one big parcel, so I won't have to grip small ones with my teeth.

Everyone wants to "cheer me up" with stories of their own afflictions. I've discovered my grocer had a bladder operation, my cheese salesman broke his collarbone, and my neighbours suffer from gout, gallstones and lower back pain.

A loud woman lined up at the Old Bagel Factory warned me of a friend "who had a little pain in his arm, and the next thing he knew he couldn't move a bone in his body.

"He died in two weeks, in terrible pain! A rare disease, the doctors said . . . I only hope you don't have the same thing."

Like everyone with a small or large handicap, I am slowly learning to use my other faculties. I open doors with my hips, I wriggle into my shirt, I kick my garbage down the stairs. I rip open envelopes and milk cartons with my teeth.

And as I struggle with my tiny injury, I pay more attention to those with real afflictions. I watch a young man in a wheelchair race by my house, pulled by a dog; and an old woman inching her way stubbornly through St. Laurent boulevard traffic. I think of Stephen Hawking, Terry Fox and Christy Brown, the hero of *My Left Foot*. And I look in embarrassment at my left arm, so helpless it can't tie my foot's shoelaces.

That is why I have decided to re-educate this long-ignored limb. Like a parent, I blame myself for my arm's inadequacies. Maybe I didn't give it enough attention in its youth, when my right arm was my obvious favourite. Perhaps it has been stigmatized by a society that refers to awkward people as "gauche."

Whatever the cause, I am going to give my left arm a fresh start. From now on, guess who gets to write my column, cook my breakfast, wash the dishes and comb my hair? Guess who makes out the mortgage payments?

The left hand is supposed to be the more creative one, linked to the creative side of the brain. Maybe my left arm has undiscovered potential — to play music, sculpt, even paint. By the time my right arm is fully recovered, it may find that it's out of a job, challenged by a mate that's learned to assert itself. I can already see a fight brewing over who takes out the garbage, who shakes other hands and who signs the checks.

I guess I'll have to find some way of dividing up the work. Pianists can do two different things at once. An octopus can do eight. Why not me?

With training, maybe I can teach my left hand to write a novel while my right hand fixes the sink, to have my left arm paint a landscape while my right one pours the drinks.

Like a modern couple, my two arms would live separate but equal lives, giving each other enough space to grow. A perfect arrangement — if I can just get them to shake on it.

V.I.P. LIKE ME

.

.

.

It was supposed to be my big night. I had made a TV film that was nominated for several Geminis, Canada's version of the Emmie Awards, and I was invited to the ceremonies as a "guest of the Academy."

True, the awards banquet took place in Toronto — not my favourite city — but it was hard to resist. Glitz. Glamour. Glory. Me — a VIP. Who could say no?

The fantasy started to unfurl the moment I got to Montreal Airport. After boarding the plane, we were delayed three hours, because Toronto Airport was clogged with traffic. By the time I left the ground, it was after 7:00 p.m. and the banquet had already started.

A white stretch limousine was waiting at Toronto airport, the driver anxious to whisk me to the dinner. "Don't worry about your baggage, sir." he said, "There's a hospitality suite at the hotel for VIP's like you. I'll drop it off there."

I would regret his generosity . . .

The awards banquet was held at the Toronto Convention Centre, a cavernous place stuffed with the luminaries of Canadian TV. Like all VIP's, I was presented with a special gift befitting my status: a shopping bag brimming with the necessities of celebrity life:

— A bottle of *Clinique Face Scrub*.
— A disposable camera.
— A gold pen in a velvet case.
— A package of "private collection" gourmet coffee.
— A plush box of chocolates, each moulded into the shape of the
   Gemini statue.

Throughout the evening the stars of Canadian TV would rarely be seen anywhere without their shopping bags. The banquet itself was a dreary affair. The invitation had asked me to dress for dancing. The dress code: "Something wild."

Wild?

I wore a white linen jacket with a green tie and sneakers — not exactly daring, but enough to keep in the spirit. I was the only person there in sneakers. Everyone else wore tuxedos or classic dark suits — wild by Toronto standards. I stuck out like a flasher at a funeral.

The liveliest event of the night was a fist fight at the next table where two guys in dark suits slugged it out, then toppled off a six-foot platform and kept wrestling on the floor, screaming things like:

"Come on big man! Show me your stuff."

When the event was over my film crew went off to eat a real dinner. I stopped by the hotel to get my bag and check in, and the night really started to turn special. Men in tuxedos were everywhere, clutching gift bags in one hand and blonde-haired women in the other. I stood at the reception desk, but was completely ignored. The receptionist alternately served "tuxedos" or did his accounting. When he started to head for the back room carrying his night-accounts book, I'd had enough. "Excuse me," I said. "My bag was left in the hospitality suite . . . How can I get it?"

"I don't know, sir," snapped the young man, his eyes travelling slowly from my white jacket to my sneakers. "I'm very busy. You'll have to go round the corner to the house phone and ask the operator to phone the suite. It's room 1500."

He left.

Five minutes and precisely 27 unanswered rings later I slammed down the phone and stormed back to the desk.

"Could you please call the room on your phone?" I asked the young man. "The operator isn't in and I'm a guest here. I've come for the Gemini awards. I just want my bag." I offered to go out for a drink and return in an hour — but the receptionist was immovable as stone.

"I'm afraid I can't help, sir," he said cooly. "Someone may be sleeping in that room and I don't want to wake them. There is nothing I can do. I'm very busy."

He returned to his accounts: I lost my temper. "Look," I declared. "Either *you* get someone to open the door . . . or I'll get it open myself."

"No you *won't!*" he snapped. "Touch that door, and I'll call the police."

It was incredible. A request for my luggage had turned into a western-style showdown. We glared across the counter at each other, waiting to see who would move first. Suddenly, a new voice broke in, from a stranger on my left. He was well-heeled, in his late-forties, short and officious.

"Young man" he barked at the receptionist. "You are completely incompetent. Get this man his baggage immediately!"

"I'm sorry sir," sniffed the receptionist. "Who are you?"

"*Who?*" said the stranger. "I *own* this building."

He threw down a card and pulled back his shoulders. "Do what I say . . . NOW."

The young man wavered. Two colossal egos were in danger of crashing like blimps.

"Remove yourself from my sight," said the newcomer icily. "GO and get this man his luggage . . . NOW!"

"Look," said the young man, pluckily trying to stand his ground. "I'll try to help, but — "

"It's okay," I broke in trying to calm things down. "Let's not go overboard . . . After all, it's only a bag."

The newcomer brushed me off like lint. He glared at the young man and pointed his finger . . .

"*Leave*. Disappear . . . . Out of my sight you incompetent. GO."

He looked at his watch, and began counting off seconds. We were at the brink of catastrophe: a confrontation between a bureaucrat and a bully. There was only one thing to do: flee. I rushed off to the elevator, abandoning the battlefield.

Room 1500. I knocked several times before a sleepy young woman answered in her nightgown. Together we ransacked the room, but there was no bag.

Back in the elevator a young bellman came up with a novel idea. As my bag was baggage, perhaps it was in the baggage room. We went off to search for it — and he was right.

Grateful, I headed back to the main desk where the receptionist was now alone, chastised. But he had a final surprise. "I'm really sorry about this, Mr. Freed, but . . ."

A special room had been reserved in my name, but somehow it had been given to someone else. They could put me up in a hospitality suite — but there was no bed. The bellman ushered me off to a room with a pull-out couch as uncomfortable as anything I've slept on in the Third World. I lay down on a thin slice of foam barely covering sagging springs and practically sank to the floor.

Grimly, I returned to the reception desk. The young man offered to try and find me a complimentary room in another hotel — but I had had enough. My crew had returned from wining and dining and one of them invited me to share his double bed.

At 3:00 a.m., exhausted, I curled up with my bedmate and dreamt of the night that should have been mine. Until the chambermaid barged in by accident at 7:30 a.m.

Tired and beaten, I packed up my white linen jacket and my bag of gifts and fled for home. The plane was two hours late; I spent the time eating all my Gemini-shaped chocolates in the airport lobby.

It was as close as I came to getting an award.

PAY NO BILLS, PLEASE

.

.

.

The worst thing about returning home from a long trip is what greets me at the door: a pile of bills I need a snow shovel to get through — a VISA bill with interest charges as large as Argentina's, a bill from the dentist threatening to repossess three fillings and a letter that starts:

"Dear Customer: Our records show that you have not settled your account with us since October, 1967 . . . although reminders have been mailed to you on 127 occasions.

"The account has no doubt escaped your notice."

To be honest, I've been a bill procrastinator ever since I was old enough to sign a cheque; never able to pay today what I can pay with interest tomorrow. I've always been awed by people who just sit right down and pay their bills — before the due date. How do they do it?

You've got to figure out what you owe, see if there's enough in your account to cover it, decide what to pay now, what to pay later. Horrible decisions: better to put them off a little longer.

What if something changes? VISA could go under between now and the time I have to pay? What if there's a municipal revolution and they have an amnesty on all parking tickets?

Why takes chances? Some companies are tougher to ignore than others, such as the phone company, which wastes little time with repeat late-payers like me.

"Dear Client: Our records show that it has been six hours since you made your last long distance phone call and we still have not received your payment.

If your bill is not settled in full by sundown today we will be forced to disconnect your phone. You will never have one again."

Consequently, I now try to take a methodical step-by-step approach to paying bills.

STEP I
When a bill arrives I lift it off the ground by the tip of my fingers as though it might electrocute me — and immediately drop it into a large basket with

my other unpaid bills. I push the basket out of sight. Psychologically, it is important to wait for the right moment to face bills (i.e. anytime but right now).

STEP 2

I keep a lookout for bills with warnings on the envelope, like PAST DUE or final notice, or URGENT! OCCUPANT BEWARE.

These are placed in another pile labelled: "Important. To be paid, eventually."

STEP 3

On the first day of every third or fourth month, I sit down and go through all my bills thoroughly. If I can find them. First, I sift through the multi-coloured garbage accompanying them: slick brochures from Bell Canada for a Laser Phone Computer Satellite Software Decoder with Extraterrestrial Dating Service, pamphlets from Hydro-Quebec proving that I "enjoy" the lowest rates in the electrified world, along with a Hydro bill that's high enough to heat a jumbo jet hangar. (That is, if I can actually figure out my new Hydro bill. It looks like Rutherford's notes for the invention of an electron-accelerator.)

STEP 4

I decide which bills must be paid promptly and which can be safely sloughed off till next month, or next year.

Tip: Before deciding, I look at the interest charges. My notary hasn't charged me a nickle interest since I last paid him in 1983; but Quebec's Revenue department charges me rates that would get the average guy jailed for loan-sharking.

This year's bill came with an easy-to-follow notice:

"Original bill: $7.35. Arrears interest $7.35 x 1.5% /month
plus carrying costs of 13 x 12 /.6785 T Y PLUS as per section c-17.
Current interest per day at rate of 234.5 /365 X T P
TOTAL BALANCE NOW OUTSTANDING: $52,731.56*

*If payment is not received by the date specified, a Quebec government representative may find it necessary to break your leg."

STEP 5

I address the envelopes and make out the cheques. Then I look frantically around and realize I have no stamps. I fold the envelopes in half and stuff them in my pocket to be mailed next time I pass a post office.

By the time I remember them again, a month has passed. By then I can safely tear them up as fresh bills have arrived in the mail.

STEP 6
I begin again at STEP 1.

NOTE: In weeks to come I will be dealing with the tricky subject of: Parking tickets and how to avoid paying them — a subject at which I have some expertise. If you have stories or ideas on this matter please forward them to:

Josh Freed
Cellblock 17
Bordeaux Jail
Montreal, P.Q.

No bills, please.

THE EARLY BIRD GETS WORMS

•

•

•

It is 7:00 a.m. and my neighbours are hard at work, hammering away on their new balcony — while I try to sleep.

There's no point in complaining. If I shout out the window, they will look at my pyjama-clad body in disgust, and chirp something like: "Early to bed, early to rise, makes a man healthy, wealthy and wise." Or "No civilized person goes to bed the same day he gets up." Then they will hammer even more loudly, convinced they are helping me build character.

Yet if I ever tried hammering outdoors at 10 o'clock at night — an hour I regard as quite reasonable — they would sic their pit bull on me and call the police.

"Are you crazy?" they would shout as the ambulance took me away bleeding. "It's the middle of the night!"

Of the many conspiracies of the self-righteous, few are as irritating as the tyranny of early morning people, and their disdain for anyone who gets up later than them.

Construction workers pound their jackhammers while it is still dark, towtrucks sound their hideous alarms as they tow my car away in the murky half-light; church bells ring, radios blare, trucks honk, dogs bark and birds sing.

Yet I dare not complain. Morning people are on the side of God; late risers are moral degenerates — criminals of the clock.

The tyranny of the early riser pervades much of society. Schools and hospitals keep the same hours as jails; trains, planes and buses always depart at dawn. Car dealers demand that I bring my car in for repairs before the sun rises; hotels stop serving breakfast just when I want to eat; government offices are closed by 4:30 — only hours after many late-risers get up.

"Up, up up! It's morning!" is the constant message. *Never let the sun shine on you in bed!*

Frankly, I have always been a late bird — even when I was forced to get up early the first seventeen years of my life. Every morning as I slept innocently, my parents would brutally tear open the bedroom curtains and drag me into the hellish nightmare of day — noise, activity, violent bright light.

For the first two hours of the school day I would sit comatose: my eyes were open, my mouth moved; few people suspected I was sound asleep. Toward the end of high school my parents gave up, convinced I was sunlight-impaired — but authorities were determined to mend my ways.

There were teachers with steely voices and two-hour detentions for "missing the bell"; camp counsellors who played reveille at dawn and woke me up with pails of ice water; stupid songs about "morning glory."

There were employers who didn't care if I was unconscious at my desk, as long as I was there.

All failed to change my natural rhythm. The truth is that I start being productive around 11 a.m. and can work cheerfully until well after midnight. As long as I can sleep in the next day.

I became a journalist because *The Montreal Star* let me come in at noon; I picked most of my friends because they stayed up late. I never moved to Toronto because they make everyone get up early.

I know that the early bird always gets the worm — but I prefer bacon and eggs. I am much happier in the dead of night than the still of morning.

Face it: Sunrise was a good time to go out and hunt for breakfast, before the advent of the grocery store. And going to bed early made a lot of sense until they discovered electricity. But the lightbulb was invented more than 100 years ago, and society has yet to catch on.

Why must we eat breakfast at eight and dinner at six, crowding every decent restaurant in town? Why must everyone go to work at the same time, clogging the highways and packing the buses? Why squeeze everything into ten brief hours — when many people would be much happier getting up late?

Frankly, I have never understood what early birds do every morning — since nothing is open yet. When I ask them they say things like: "I take a brisk walk, I listen to the birds. I plan my day."

Like most night owls I prefer evening movies to early walks, late-night dinners to power breakfasts. I prefer gazing at the moon to blinking in the sun — at least it doesn't cause cancer.

I hate talk shows in the morning because the people on them are smarter than I am at that hour; I hate hospitals that wake you up at dawn — when there is absolutely nothing to do.

I hate people who phone early and say: "Sorry. Did I wake you?" I know that secretly, they hope they did.

I once experienced an early morning in winter and it was frightening indeed. The sky was dark and cold, the streets filled with cheerless zombies, lurching to work like Frankensteins in the wintry half-light. Far better to get up when the air is warm, the sky is bright and the buses empty. Better to sleep late and skip rush hour. But where is the saying that goes:

Rise at noon, work till night.
And you can beat the traffic light.

If you ask me, the only reason early birds still dominate society is because they're up too early for anyone to stop them. I suspect that secretly, many early birds would prefer to rise later than they do — which is why they resent those of us who do.

Well, don't worry. When I run the world, your schedule will change. Schools will start at noon and end at 6:00 p.m. for youngsters like me who peaked late; work will start precisely 90 minutes after whenever you decide to get up. Lunch won't start until 3:00 p.m. — because it's horrible for a late riser to come to work when everyone else is going off to eat. And all noise will be illegal before 10:00 a.m. — except for the sound of newspapers rustling and coffee gently percolating.

The truth is that early mornings are bad for your health. Take it from me, and James Thurber, who wrote:

Early to rise,
Early to bed
Makes a man healthy,
Wealthy and dead.

THE HOLE TRUTH

•

•

•

Like all horrible things, it began innocuously: a slip of paper lying in the doorway when I arrived home late one night. It was a notice from Gaz Metropolitain, the natural gas company.

"In order to serve you better . . . ," it began, and went on to outline repair work in the area "to install new gas lines . . . respecting localization specifications."

Too complicated to figure out at 2:00 a.m., I thought, trotting off to sleep; I'd read it in the morning.

K-RANGH-GHU-u-u-u-uhhnnnh . . . K-K-K-RANGHHHUUnnnnh.

It was a sound from hell, yet it seemed to be *in* my bedroom. Worse, it didn't go away when I opened my eyes. I leapt from bed and rushed to the window.

Not 10 feet away was an enormous backhoe, smashing its shovel on the sidewalk like a hungry bird demanding food. Other machines lined the street, sounding a similar reveille for my neighbours. The noise was deafening.

It was 6:30 a.m.

As my ears became attuned, I could make out other sounds amid the din: a small generator nearby, making whining noises: *Mnnnuuuhhh . . . Mnnuuu u-h-hh . . . Mnnnuuuuhhhhh.* A truck backing up, emitting a shrill warning cry: *Beepbeepbeepbeepbeep.*

In the distance, a cacophony of other sounds — crashing, pounding, grating — too ghastly to reproduce. I am a night bird. I work late and sleep in. 6:30 a.m. is the middle of my night.

I stepped out into the street. Machines and men swarmed everywhere. Most of the men wore green helmets and ear protectors; others wore white hats and barked orders. They were busily assuring my neighbours that it was all for our own good. The work *had* to be done; it would only last several days.

Several days?

The first wave of the invasion lasted more than a week, a military occupation involving 150 men in four teams, 40 trucks and 50 other machines that bounced up and down making snickering sounds: *Chuh-chuh-chuh — chuh-chuh-chuh*

Reluctantly, the neighbourhood adapted. I started to sleep on the sofa in the back room. I grew accustomed to an 8-foot deep moat in the middle of the street that most of kids in the area quickly preferred to the park.

Dust was everywhere, noises constant, parking impossible. We left our cars on adjacent streets, illegally, assuming that that would be tolerated in the circumstances. In the first four days, I had three parking tickets.

Yet this was only Phase 1 of the nightmare. Phase 2 began when the men in white hats began ringing doors telling residents they would have to do a "little digging" in our gardens. A few hours later, giant machines were squatting in our yards, tearing out 10-foot clumps of earth. Many of my neighbours had been working in their gardens for over a month. Appalled, one of them complained that he had planted Boston lilies — smuggled in from the U.S. — nurtured carefully over four years.

"Don't worry," said a man in a white hat. "We'll just dig a tiny hole."

When my neighbour returned from work, his garden was a bottomless crater, all sign of the lilies expunged. Pansies and petunias, tomatoes, turnips and tulips — all met the same fate, buried alive by men in construction boots. My Portuguese neighbour wears a black dress and speaks neither English nor French. She lives for her garden, a small plot of vegetables she tends like a mother.

When the earth mover showed up she had to be dragged away by her family. "The shoots are just coming up," she cried out in Portuguese, but the men did not understand. They left an eight-foot trough in her garden, shaped like a grave.

"Every district we go, people complain," a white hat confided. "They don't understand that they're fighting something bigger than them. They're fighting the power of the *government*."

He stroked his moustache thoughtfully. "People buy a house and they think: 'That's it. It's mine . . . My home.' But there's no such thing as your home. The government can do what it wants."

Now we are in the final days of destruction. As I write, most of the moat has been filled in and the road has been re-surfaced. A new machine is going up and down the street, making dust and a new noise: *Pooka pooka pooka pooka pooka.*

Phase 3 is complete: Phase 4 remains. We are told that a city landscaper took photos of our street before the invasion. According to the white hats, the landscaper will reproduce everything exactly as it was. But scepticism prevails.

How can you reproduce a budding shoot? A four week-old tomato?

What if the pictures get mixed up? Will my neighbour with the Boston lilies find he has inherited the Portuguese tomato patch? Will the Portuguese woman get the lilies, or the Italian family's roses. Who will get the Solomon seals?

We stay tuned for the final chapter, unwilling participants in our tiny soap opera. The white hats say they will be gone in days — but it no longer seems as important. Like earthquake victims, our psyches have been scarred, our innocence shattered. From now on, no matter how clear the sky, how quiet the day, the presence of the white hats will hang in the air like rain about to fall. We are poised for the sound of their return:

Mnnnuuuuuuuuuuuhhhhhhhhhh.

DR. FREED AND MR. WALSH

•
•
•

My unusual relationship with M. Walsh dates back several years — though I never imagined how far things would go. I'd been getting a lot of crank phone calls and wanted my number removed from the phonebook. But when I called Bell Canada, an operator told me the new "service" would cost me several dollars — every month.

"I have to pay for *not* being listed?" I asked.

"Yes, sir," said the operator. "Unless someone else in your household will be listed in your place."

"Someone else?" I said, thinking aloud. "You mean if I put another name in the phonebook instead of mine, there's no monthly charge?"

"That's correct . . . As long as the person resides at your address."

"Well, then put down my roomate's name," I declared, searching the air for a suitable name. "It's uhhh . . . Mr. Walsh."

"His first initial, sir?" said the operator.

"M." I replied.

Thus was born M. Walsh, a non-person who has shared my phone number for several years, and slowly infiltrated my life. Soon after the next phonebook came out, I started getting mail addressed to M. Walsh. At first I was embarrassed to open it — I don't usually read other people's mail — but as it piled up in the hallway, I couldn't resist.

A foundation for cancer wanted to know if M. Walsh would donate money; a cooking magazine wanted him to subscribe. Most interesting was an invitation to purchase THE BOOK OF WALSH's: "a unique opportunity to discover the Walsh family tree" — illustrious members of M. Walsh's family living everywhere from Australia to the arctic.

There were phone calls for Walsh too. Real estate brokers wanted to know if he owned his house and was interested in selling.

A fast-talking saleswoman wanted him to make his "pre-funeral arrangements" — including a will, a coffin and a plot — while he was still young enough to "afford the best."

There were personal calls too, like the woman who left a whiskey-slurred message on my answering machine. "I know you moved Marty, but you can't get out of my life that easy. I love ya . . . I do . . . I really do."

Hoping to give Walsh a low profile, I didn't answer his calls or mail. But when *The Globe and Mail* called with a special introductory half-price offer, I couldn't resist. J. Freed had already taken the *Globe* offer and was no longer eligible — so I took a subscription out in Walsh's name.

We paid his bill promptly and from then on Walsh's reputation seemed to grow. As word of his reading habits spread, other journals called: a new business magazine, *Maclean's*, and *The Montreal Gazette*. There were book societies and record companies, a credit card offer from Sunoco, invitations to join auto clubs, airline clubs and more:

"Start with $1000 and earn $400,000 in three years, Mr. Walsh," offered a personalized brochure. "You can become a millionaire without even trying."

Reader's Digest sent a "special sweepstakes" card marked "Confidential . . . for M. Walsh." It read:

"I don't mind telling you that it's not everyone in Montreal who gets a chance to enter the *Reader's Digest* $550,000 "lifetime security" sweepstakes — but this month the Walsh home in Quebec was placed on our entry list.

"Congratulations. You have come through the first two stages in our sweepstakes."

The Red Cross sent a personalized note asking Walsh to identify the "many mortal risks" at his Esplanade avenue residence. Were his carpets well-fixed on the floor to avoid slipping? Were his night clothes inflammable? Did he wear safety glasses when he mowed the lawn?

As his stature rose, polling houses started to call too — never for me, only for Walsh.

"How many beers a day do you drink?" asked a pollster for the provincial health department. She wanted M. Walsh, but he wasn't in — so I answered for him, as usual.

"Two," I said. After years of living with Walsh I felt I knew him as well as myself.

"How many glasses of wine?" asked the pollster.

"Two or three," I replied "but only with dinner."

Did Walsh go to the racetrack, asked a pollster for the Minister of Revenue. Did he buy 6-49 lottery tickets? Bet on sports pools? Play bingo?

Yes, I answered to every question. I don't gamble myself — but I am sure Walsh is a betting man.

Lately, political pollsters have been calling regularly, eager to know Walsh's voting preference in the next provincial election.

"Still undecided," I told them again last month. But it wasn't enough.

"Which issue is more important," they demanded "— language or hospitals?"

"The language of hospitals," I replied, before hanging up. Walsh is a complex man.

Frankly, my double-life as M. Walsh is starting to get to me. In recent months, as I read Walsh's mail, listen to his messages, answer his questionnaires, I feel I am living more and more vicariously.

Since J. Freed is not listed in the phonebook, he is never asked his opinion by pollsters, rarely solicited by mail, except for the *Reader's Digest* Sweepstakes. He rarely even gets any phone calls, except from a few souls who recall his number from the days he was listed.

Slowly, Freed is fading away, a shell of a person who shows up occasionally in the media and cadges off Walsh's phone listing. Like Dr. Jekyll, I am being replaced — by Mr. Walsh, the guy who gets all my mail.

Last week, Walsh really came into his own. He received a personalized letter from American Express, offering him a credit card. It read as follows:

RESERVED FOR M. WALSH . . . PRIVILEGED STATUS:

"To say it all . . . the American Express card isn't made for everyone, and it is not sufficient to ask for one to get it.

"Thus, I announce with great pleasure that American Express has accorded you with privileged status . . . a mark of confidence in which you can truly be proud.

"Thanks to privileged status, you are now part of a restricted group of people for whom the request for a card has every chance of being approved."

Not bad for a person whose total lifetime purchases amount to a 13-week subscription to *The Globe and Mail*.

Not surprisingly, Walsh has decided to take the card while it's being offered. He feels it's time to come out of the closet and enjoy his new-found status — despite the obvious drawbacks. Once Walsh gets his new American Express card, he knows more offers will pour in by mail and phone. And he doesn't want just anyone to call.

So Walsh has decided to get an unlisted number. To avoid paying the extra charge to the telephone company, he's going to list his phone under somebody else's name — someone innocuous, who hasn't been offered Privileged Status — his roommate — Mr. Freed.

* M. Walsh's name has been altered, to protect his privacy.

CANADIAN AUTOMOBILE
TRILOGY : 2

•
•
•

Josh Freed
Montreal
June 2, 1990

Dear Vandal:

"For several years now you have shared my car with me. I use it during the day; you abuse it during the night. I buy car parts; you steal them."

So began a letter I wrote to you last August, describing my growing distress over our relationship. At the time you had stolen four mirrors, two tail-lights, one tapedeck, half a headrest and part of my back bumper. I was considering hanging out a sign saying "Freed Auto Parts."

I told you I had gone from anger to homicidal rage and finally despair. I said it was time to terminate our affair. Who knew it had just begun?

In the ten months since I wrote that letter, you have entered my life with incredible zeal, visiting more frequently than my friends. And your appetite has grown.

Several weeks after I wrote you, my outside mirror disappeared again ($134), followed quickly by a door handle ($38.30), the back wiper ($36.20) and the chrome fitting around my bumper ($82). Other days you were more playful: You scratched decorative markings on my front hood ($139) and punched a hole in the back of my trunk ($247).

Strangely, the more you stole or mangled my car the less angry I became. How many times can you mourn?

I started to approach my car each morning with foreboding. Which hubcap would be missing? What part smashed? I was practically disappointed if everything was intact. Unfortunately, I had to pay for parts myself — because my insurance company had raised my deductible. You'd vandalized my car so often they were including you in calculating my risk. You had become my dependent.

I grew paranoid. I live on a normal street full of normal-looking cars.

Why was mine the only one being hunted? Was it the model: a European car police say is the rage among Quebec vandals? Or did you just like the colour — burgundy?

Was there something about my car in particular that obsessed you?: An automotive version of *Fatal Attraction*? Was it cursed with bad "karma"? — a vehicle that had been vandalized in earlier lives as a stagecoach and a Roman chariot?

Or was it me you hated? Could you be a critic of my column? Had I somehow offended you? Maybe you just didn't like my face. In March you suffered a crisis: a violent attack of vandalism that left behind a trail of missing or mutilated parts. I amused some friends by arriving for a dinner party holding my car's entire front grill ($97). I'd found it lying beside my driver's door, like an omen. Foolishly, I replaced it, and days later, it was gone again — with both my front headlights ($898).

I searched desperately for a garage to park my car overnight, but there was nothing in my area — so I took other precautions. I parked in front of my house and peeked outside every half hour. I fell asleep later and later; lost more and more sleep.

For six weeks, my vigilance worked. You took nothing: no mirrors, no bumpers, not even a door handle. I thought we'd come to a truce — until last Saturday.

You took my car ($14,254).

It's strange when an object that big simply disappears. At first I thought I'd misplaced it, like my keys. I searched the street for hours convinced it must be there. I sat in a police car, spilling out my guts as if to a psychiatrist.

The cop didn't comfort me: he said my car had probably skipped town and headed for Florida — but I didn't believe him. I was certain you had only borrowed it to remove some larger parts; you'd return it any day, without the engine.

Yesterday, I finally came to grips with the truth: My car isn't coming home. I have been the victim of a psychotic serial car-part vandal, whose lust for parts knew no bounds.

So why am I writing to you? The truth is that I need a favour. I want to buy another car — but this time I'd like one of my own. So I'd thought I'd better get your advice.

Will you vandalize any car I buy, or just certain models? Can you recommend a simple car, one that might not tempt you? A Lada? A second-hand truck? Or should I stick to a bicycle?

Please write me anonymously. For three years I have dutifully served as a donor bank for car-part organs. I have given you dozens of parts worth thousands of dollars, with little complaint.

I have made the ultimate sacrifice and ask little in return.

P.S. To other readers. Be advised: If you see a burgundy Volkswagen *Golf* on the street, with licence number JDM 064, please call me. But feel free to take a piece for yourself. I'm used to it.

Josh

Natural Life

WHITHER THE WEATHER

.

.

.

There was a time when people who talked about the weather were considered boring. These days few of us talk about anything else. As the climate becomes increasingly unpredictable, we become more and more dull. Turn on the radio and there's a weather forecast every ten minutes — aimed at growing numbers of weather junkies who change their clothing whenever the sun goes behind a cloud.

Papers like *USA Today* print weather maps as big as Rhode Island, and make the daily forecast sound like World War III.

"In the southern plains, dry air is clashing with humid air to produce dangerous thunderstorms," said a recent *USA Today* story. "Across Iowa, warm and cold air are also battling." Environment Canada has a Weatherline you call to get the weather and a weather office where you call to complain.

Then there's TV weather: an incomprehensible mush of satellite photos and space-age jargon you need a meteorology degree to decipher.

I've been watching the weather most of my life and I still don't know what the barometric pressure is — let alone why I need to know it. I'm sure it's very important to sailors — but why can't they buy a barometer? And what difference does it make if 35 kilometre winds come from the southwest — instead of the northeast? Either way, I need a sweater.

There was a time when predicting the weather was simple: you recited something about *red sky at morning, sailor's warning* — and stuck your hand out the window. If it got wet you put on a raincoat. Things changed with the arrival of CBC's first weatherman — Percy Saltzman — the original Canadian weather personality. I vaguely recall a small, bespectacled man who looked like my algebra teacher drawing squiggly clouds in chalk on a blackboard, and enthusing:

"Well . . . it sure looks like sun tomorrow!!! . . . Unless clouds move in."

Then he'd throw the chalk in the air — the closest thing to special effects back then — and say:

"And that's the weather!"

Today the blackboard has been replaced by swirling satellite photos that look like the inside of someone's stomach. Percy himself has been dumped for young fashion plates in pleated suits and pressed hair who point at the stomach photos and say:

"The maximum minimum tomorrow is 12 with a precipitation factor of 26.2 and a high-pressure system in Baie Comeau causing a low-pressure trough in Ste. Agathe and flooding in Papua New Guinea."

They give us the short-term forecast, good for the next 10 minutes, the long term forecast, good for the next decade; they tell us the temperature in Auckland, Zimbabwe and Myrtle Beach. (Where exactly is Myrtle Beach and why do I keep hearing its weather?)

When they aren't telling me what the weather will be, they're telling me what it used to be.

"The hottest day in North America on this date was in Death Valley in 1913 — 57 degrees. The hottest day in the world was 59 degrees in El Azizia Libya."

They give the visibility report for pilots, the marine report for submarine captains, and the odds on the weather for bookies.

"Chances of precipitation are 92%; chances of fog 37.3%. Betting closes in ten minutes."

It's all baffling. No sooner do I master one term than they invent a new one. Just when I'd figured out that "precipitation" really meant rain, Environment Canada suddenly introduced something called the "Humidex Alert."

If this Humidex Alert broke 40, they warned, we should curtail all outdoor activities, run to the nearest air-conditioner, and suck. As best I can follow, it's really some kind of danger index for people with heart problems.

What next? . . . A radiation report for people with pacemakers? The acid rain count — to indicate if you need a lead umbrella?

The Ultraviolet Index? ("We recommend a No. 38 sunblock today.")

This meteorological madness will probably get worse, given the latest weapon in the arsenal of the climate junkie, the all-weather channel, providing "all of the weather, all of the time."

Quebec's weather station only started up a couple of years ago and is still a bit tacky. It plays an interminable tape of Vivaldi's "Four Seasons," while a nervous young woman points at pictures of cloud cover over Kapuskasing.

But much more will soon be on the way, if you go by the weather channel in the U.S. There, aspiring young Dan Rathers in $2200 suits strut around before holograph photos of satellite stomachs, giving up-to-the-minute weather reports everywhere from the Sahara to the North Pole.

There are Drought Reports and Tidal Reports. There is the hourly Weather News — dedicated entirely to disasters caused by climate: monsoon deaths in Bangladesh, hurricane destruction in Fiji, Hydro blackouts in Quebec . . .

"We take you now to Cairo for the daily Sand Count."

Regional, national and international weather are followed by planetary conditions and the galactic report.

"And in the Milky Way, some solar storms coming up followed by meteor showers, sun flares and asteroid hail."

"Mars is having a chilly day but Mercury is once again *very* hot. And now — the Intergalactic Forecast."

Last summer I stayed at a small inn in Massachusetts, where it rained every day for a week. The innkeeper spent the entire time glued to the weather channel, vicariously living through Asian droughts and Arctic blizzards she would never get to experience first-hand. Like many Americans she didn't know much about geography — but she sure knew her weather.

She couldn't find Europe on a map, but she knew the precipitation count in Ulan Bator, the temperature spread in Tierra del Fuego, the humidity in Bahrein.

"My lord, look how hot it is in Tamil Nadu," she'd say. "It's terrible, terrible — even worse than in Sudan. I'm sure glad that I don't live in one of those mid-west states."

Yet despite the insidious spread of all-weather stations and services, one thing is reassuring. For all the sophistication of today's weather — the windchill factors and humidex alerts, the satellite stomachs and space-age terminology spouted by experts in silk suits — at least one thing hasn't changed since the days of Percy Saltzman.

Tomorrow's weather forecast is usually wrong.

WITH APOLOGY TO ECOLOGY

•

•

•

"THE GREENHOUSE EFFECT IS HERE! You must realize by now that our summers are getting longer and hotter. Why put it off?"

— Advertisement for air conditioners. *Montreal Gazette*, August 9, 1989.

Everywhere I turn, people are talking about the Greenhouse Effect. TV news credits it for everything from droughts to floods; my neighbours blame it for rain, sleet, hail and sun. Newspaper features say it's behind marital disputes, heart attacks, nervous breakdowns and homicide.

What's going on? After years of lunching on the environment, it's starting to lunch on us.

Like most people I hadn't thought much about the "effect" until the recent heat wave. I know winter has been getting warmer, but who's going to complain about shovelling *less* snow?

The recent hot spell has finally got me worried. My house has been so hot that my cactus wilted. Friends of mine have been sleeping on the porch; others have moved into an air-conditioned motel.

And the rain: monsoon-like storms that flash through the city like hurricanes — leaving it *just* as hot afterwards. There was one that hit town recently. The thunder and lightning would have done justice to Armageddon.

Those were TREES lying on the ground afterward. What next? Earthquakes? Tidal waves? A plague of locusts? I don't need a 15-foot alligator walking in my front door to convince me that this *isn't* the climate I grew up in.

Doomsday scenarios abound: the prairies will turn into a desert; New York City will flood and join Atlantis; Montreal will wind up in the tropics, the St. Lawrence river rising so fast you'll need a boat to get to work. According to honchos at Environment Canada, it's time we took steps to "mitigate some of the adverse effects" of the Greenhouse Effect — so I'm taking their advice. If Montreal is going to become the New Delhi of North America, why not be prepared? Here are some suggestions:

✦ Look for a new house, on high ground. When the monsoon season arrives and flooding starts — you can be sure the City of Montreal won't foot the bill. Some place like the peak of Mont Tremblant should be a safe location. You won't be pestered by crowds of noisy, colour-coordinated skiers; there won't be skiing anymore.

✦ As the "hot season" settles in, you won't want to be on the fiery Gangetic plain surrounding Montreal. The British Raj used to flee to cool "hill stations" in Kashmir; you should consider a similar country retreat. Now is a good time to buy land on Baffin Island — where prices are cheap and swimming should soon be quite warm.

✦ Develop some useful new skills, like cultivating orange trees and mango groves, or cutting your way through dense jungle vines with a machete.

✦ The good news from Environment Canada is that some northern areas will soon make excellent agricultural land. Think about buying a small farm in James Bay, as soon as Quebec gets smart and stops flooding the future "breadbasket of the north."

✦ Study up on exotic animal life. You'll be saying goodbye to the bushy-tailed squirrel, the fox and the bear, and hello to new friends — like the iguana, the lizard and the boa-constrictor. If raising animals interests you, look into a crocodile farm on Lake Erie.

✦ Finally, tourism will offer excellent business opportunities. As the U.S. becomes a desert wasteland, millions of fun-seeking Southerners will be flocking to our northern Disneyland.

You could lead glass-bottom boat trips through the piranha-infested swamps of the Lachine Canal; or offer guided tours up a newly-active volcano, Mount Royal, to see the monkeys and panthers.

However, if you plan to open a tourist shop, remember that shopping hours will probably change — to avoid the heat of the day and allow for siesta. Figure on store hours of, say, 6:00-9:00 a.m., and 4:00-7:00 in the afternoon.

There are some sober souls who suggest a more cautious approach to the Greenhouse Effect. They say we should think ecologically. Cut down on car air-conditioning. Eliminate damaging aerosol sprays. Use less gas, coal and oil and more wind, hydro, and solar power — since they don't contribute to the greenhouse effect. Conserve energy.

But that would take a lot of personal energy, and frankly, I've got no time to spare. I've just started to build an ark. When it comes to the environment, you can't be too careful.

BAN THAT TAN

•

•

•

OK, kids. Before you go outside I want you to bundle up, put on your hats and get out your umbrellas . . . . It's sunny outside.

This summer, there's something new under the sun — sunblock. A day at the beach used to mean slathering on the cooking oil and barbecuing yourself until your skin was charred. In the evening you smeared intensive-care vaseline all over your body and figured you had a good base for a *real* tan.

Serious sun worshippers supplemented their tan with sun-lamps and aluminum reflectors — the microwave ovens of the suntanning world — or just toasted their skin lightly with a match. But things are changing fast. As fear spreads about the ozone layer, the Greenhouse Effect and skin cancer, the sun is starting to get a bad name. Sunshine is becoming as unfashionable as cigarettes.

It's time to ban the tan.

Up at my lake in the Laurentians last week, most people were sitting under trees or umbrellas and saying things like: "I already got my ten minutes of sun this morning."

I tried to go out swimming and an older woman *ordered* me to put on a hat — in the water!

"Don't you know that's where the rays are most dangerous?" she lectured, as I joined a lakeful of bald men swimming in soggy hats. Several people were wearing special $200 sunglasses to "keep out the ultraviolet rays." Others had smeared a rust-coloured zinc cream all over their noses.

Parents had covered their toddlers in sun-bonnets and sunblock no. 60 and ordered them to come inside immediately if the sun came out from behind a cloud.

"The sun is no longer our friend," seemed to be the new parental message. "This is a new sun — an evil sun."

While the anti-sun movement has just come into fashion, it hasn't surprised my old buddy — Deep Shade — a guy who's been hiding from the sun since he was old enough to squint. Deep Shade avoids direct sunlight like a mole. He dresses in billowy robes, stays off balconies and only takes walks at night. At the sea-shore he sits fully-clothed beneath a tree, under an umbrella.

We spoke down in his garage, as always, because that's where he spends most of the summer. His skin was as white as marshmallow.

"Stay away from sun-decks, skylights and sandy beaches," he warned sternly. "And *never* eat on an outdoor restaurant-terrace . . . It's so hot the mayonnaise in your sandwich curdles before it gets to your table.

"Everyone's crammed in like sardines, sweating, squinting and inhaling diesel fumes. And saying: 'Oh, isn't this lovely?'

"Go inside where it's air-conditioned. The best seats in the house are empty."

Deep Shade points out that the desire for a sun-tan is a recent aberration in a long history of people trying to stay pale. Until this century dark skin meant you were a working stiff, forced to toil outside in the fields. Light skin was a sign of the upper classes, who rarely ventured outside without a parasol. It was only after World War II that the suntan became a rage — a sign that you were rich enough to lie around the beach. Suddenly burnt skin was in, showed off by skimpy clothing like the bikini — appropriately named after Bikini Atoll, site of the first thermonuclear test blast.

Suntan lotion was invented in the 1940s, encouraging people to bake until they were bronze, turning slowly in the sun, like barbecue chicken in a rotisserie.

At last, says Deep Shade, the pendulum is swinging back. Sun-tan lotion has given way to sun-screen and sun-block. A "nice healthy tan" is suddenly associated with wrinkles and skin disease.

"Marcia — You're so *dark!* Maybe you should see a doctor."

"What next?" I asked Deep Shade, and he smiled with glee.

"Sun-decks and sun-roofs are going out of style . . . along with Sunkist oranges and sun-dried tomatoes."

As the sun goes out of fashion, he explained, so will the products that came with it. Coppertone will vanish, replaced with Milky Way (in the commercial the dog will pull down a girl's bathing suit, revealing her back is as white as her rear).

People who have to work outdoors will be wrapped in protective suits and goggles, like welders exposed to dangerous light. Household design will transform. Rooms will be painted dark green like they were before everyone renovated them. Windows will be bricked over or covered with dark curtains and blinds. Lofts will be out, basement apartments will be the rage.

"Bright rooms will be seen as depressing. Dark rooms will be in, associated with health and happiness."

As the sun becomes our enemy, our entire psychology will shift. School kids will no longer draw pictures of a house with a big smiling sun in the corner; this will be considered morbid. The sun will wear a nasty, malevolent frown. Well-adjusted kids will leave the sun out of the picture entirely and replace it with big smiling clouds. To go with nursery rhymes that say:

"Sun, sun, go away, come again another day."

And pop songs like: *"You are my cloudburst, my only cloudburst."*

Or *"You are the raincloud of my life."*

Even our vocabulary will change. Having a "sunny" temperament will mean being gloomy and morose. Cheerful people will have a cloudy disposition, and always look at the "dark side of things." Wrapped in long blankets they will sit smeared in sunblock no. 600 under their asbestos umbrellas smiling at the weather forecast.

"Good news folks . . . A heavy cloudfront is rolling in from the north . . . . Time to put away those umbrellas and soak up some rain."

BATTLE OF THE BUG
(WHEN MAN MEETS MOSQUITO)

.

.

.

I am Upnorth in the country perched on my verandah, gazing at the lake, smelling the flowers and flailing my arms like a windmill. It is bug season, pitting man against mosquito, and the patios of cottage-owners run red with blood — their own.

The brief Canadian summer is supposedly a time to forget the winter's hardship; a time for hot sun and warm water, long drinks and short pants. A time for Upnorth. Yet while we hate to admit it, the Canadian countryside isn't the paradise it's cracked up to be. It is an elaborate self-deception: a struggle from start to finish.

To get there you must battle hordes of cottage-starved drivers, each ready to kill to start relaxing five minutes ahead of the next car. You must also stew in hours of stalled traffic, because construction crews save all major repair work for summer weekends.

And when you finally arrive at the cottage, frazzled and ready to flop, your houseguests are already there, eagerly awaiting you. While you've been fattening yourself up in the city, they have been on a starvation diet, preparing for a weekend feast — and you are on the menu.

The guest list will include:

THE BLACKFLY: The first arrival of summer season, it is the pit bull of the insect world, a vicious creature as tiny as a pinhead, with a bite that looks like an extra-large pizza. It is often accompanied by microscopic "no-see-ums" — though unfortunately, they see you and you feel-'em.

THE MOSQUITO: The B-52 of the bug kingdom, the mosquito's buzz is worse than its bite. Its appearance is no better: a mass of quivering limbs, eerie antennae and spindly parts too disgusting to contemplate — especially when it is sipping on your blood.

THE DEERFLY: A recent Upnorth vacationer, this large fly-like creature has the bite of an axe and an IQ to match. It drones about your head for hours, no matter how often you swing at it; eventually it will bite you so savagely you will howl with pain and kill it instantly — but its relatives will arrive minutes later and exact revenge.

A host of other bugs will also visit: humungous horseflies that tear the flesh off your body, sadistic wasps that sting you for fun, giant mutant bumblebees, samurai hornets and creepy-looking things like dragonflies that don't even have to bite. They scare you to death by appearance alone.

All told, there are 90,000 species of bug life in North America, and, as a horror film trailer might say: *THEY ARE COMING YOUR WAY.*

In our urban foolishness, we try to fight them off with a battery of anti-bug artillery: lotions and potions, bug sprays and bug juice. But it is all futile: most bugs consider these hors d'oeuvres before the main course.

Yesterday, my tiny Upnorth community, near Ste. Agathe, looked like an armed camp. No one had stepped outside since we started the barbecue and found the black flies had eaten the steak — and part of the grill.

Toxic coils and peststrips dangled from every tree, deadly vapours hung in the air. Periodically, you could hear the sizzle of high-voltage gadgets frying bugs alive — entomology's answer to the electric chair.

It was the Belfast of the bug world.

Inside our house, my family was crouched in fear, lathered, in *6-12* and *Off*, counting bites. My father had just been bitten by a wasp, in the living room, and everyone was armed with magazines, exchanging advice:

"Don't bathe: dirt scares black flies away. Always wear dull clothing: mosquitoes love bold spring colours. *Never* use shampoo."

I was the only person within miles who was actually outside, testing a recent product on the anti-bug hotline: Bounce — the fabric softener you throw in the wash to soften sheets. Apparently, when placed on your head, strips of Bounce will drive off biting bugs, so I'd bought some on the way Upnorth. I hung a strip under my hat, dangled some others from my belt and my socks — then stepped outside. For several minutes, I didn't get a single bite: the bugs were too busy laughing at me.

Eventually, they closed in for the kill and I retreated inside to count my wounds, as always. For in truth, there is no defense against the armies of the bite. Bugs are as resilient a part of Canadian life as rocks, trees and snow. And they don't get their due in our national folklore.

Look at Canada's coins and what do you see? The moose. The loon. The beaver. Be honest: When was the last time *you* saw a beaver?

It's time our national symbols reflected the life we live in this savage, thankless land, the challenge we face to eke out a simple summer weekend.

Let's put a deerfly on the quarter. A blackfly on the nickle. A no-see-'um on the dime. Let's remove the insipid maple leaf from the flag and replace it with something that means something to us: a huge red mosquito, swollen with the blood of the Canadian cottage-dweller.

A national symbol with bite.

SCAT

.

.

.

Yesterday I was chatting with my grocer, an aging, grumpy Eastern-European who works constantly and never smiles. Suddenly, he heard a sound and leapt up in concern.

"Excuse me," he said, scurrying away from the cash. "She needs me! I have to go."

"Who," I asked, worried. "Is your wife sick?"

"No," he said, and broke into a sheepish grin. "My cat — she meowed . . . . she's hungry."

To my chagrin, my grocer is a cat lover: one of untold millions who feed and fawn over their felines — getting little in return. Otherwise intelligent people, they have been mesmerized and manipulated by a sycophantic ball of fur. They will stroke their cats' bellies for hours at a time, clean out their litter-boxes like janitorial help, pay for manicures and meals. In the words of my grocer:

"I give her food and housing, lifetime medical care and old age pension . . . and she doesn't have to do nothing in return — just be happy!

"She exploits me, she exploits me," he says with a sigh and smiles contentedly. "I love her."

Just how the cat has pulled off this scam has always been a mystery to me. Especially when you compare it to the other well-known pet of our time — the dog. Feed and board a dog and it is yours forever, a faithful vassal at your beck and call — loyal, grovelling, obedient. Exactly the kind of treatment you want when you're paying the bills.

Do the same for your cat and it could care less. Step into the house and you can hear it thinking:

"Hey, great. The sucker's home again . . . . Meow (food please)! Meow! (open the window, I want to take a walk). OK, now . . . scratch my belly.

"MMMmmmmmmeow . . . OK, thanks for nothing, sucker. Now buzz off . . . It's time for my nap."

Come home to a dog and its thinking is totally different.

"The door! . . . Ohboyohboyohboy!! It's hi-i-mmmmm! (gallop gallop gallop).
The meal ticket! (drool drool drool). My best friend (slobber slobber slobber).
"Ohboyohboyohboy!! . . . Maybe he'll let me get his slippers!"

And dogs are smart. They fetch the paper and guard the house, lick your hand, and do all kinds of other useful tricks — like walking on their hind legs while carrying a tennis ball. A good dog will leap through the picture window to greet you at the front door. Incredibly, it loves you more than you love yourself.

What does a cat do — apart from groom itself? Slaughter birds? Smother babies? Claw guests? I have seen cat owners bandaged to the neck, trying to conceal gaping wounds. Ask what happened and they'll shrug and say:

"My cat scratched me — but it's nothing. She's been moody lately . . . . I'm worried about her."

Cats have been making suckers out of humans for a long time. The ancient Egyptians were the first people to be domesticated by the cat, actually worshipping the cat as a sacred animal. They buried them in special cat cemeteries, embalmed them in expensive cat clothing, mummified them in bronze cat casks — along with dead mice, in case they got hungry in the afterlife.

Other nationalities weren't much smarter. Confucius had a favourite cat; Mohammed preached with one in his arms. The Japanese had cats guarding their sacred manuscripts — probably the only time in history a cat has had to work for a meal.

During the Middle Ages, cats fell briefly out of favour — burned as witches by the thousands (Some say the plague started because there were no cats to catch the rats.) But by the Renaissance the cat was back in fashion, and today it is the pet of our times. Sadly, polls show the cat has usurped the dog as humankind's best friend.

The dog's steadfast loyalty is dismissed as stupidity, its affection as mere drooling, its party tricks as servility. Draconian laws force dog owners to trail behind their pets with a shovel and bag.

The cat has become the pet for the 1980s — the perfect size for a one-room condo, discrete enough not to disturb the neighbours, as elegant as a piece of art. An uncommitted animal for uncommitted times.

So what if cats don't apprehend criminals, save drowning kids, sniff out heroin, track down missing people or whimper at their master's grave. So what if they disappear for days and return only to use the kitty-litter, before leaving again, like a teenager borrowing his parent's car.

If a spaceship of aliens arrived to study earth, they would think cats ruled the planet by hypnotic power. Why else would the world's hardest-working species slavishly cater to a useless creature?

Fortunately, I am immune to the cat's charms. Why? I am allergic to them. When I pet a cat I sneeze and wheeze; my skin breaks out in a rash. This has no influence on my ill feelings for the cat, of course. It's just that through my watery eyes, I am the only person able to see cats clearly.

BLACK CHRISTMAS

.

.

.

T'was the night before Christmas
And all through the town,
Not a creature was stirring
Without sheepskin or down.

Outside was a desert of ice, sleet and snow
And the mercury hovered 'round 60 below.
The townsfolk lay shivering, awake in their beds,
While visions of beach bums danced in their heads.

The city was empty, few souls could be seen,
Nothing but towtrucks, hauling cars to Lachine.
The Green Onions too, they were on overtime,
Looking for stationary wheelchairs to fine.

In the distance, the Big O it gleamed in the night,
Reminding Quebecers of their yearly tax bite.
And in every window, the candles were out,
In case of a Christmas Eve power blackout.

As for me, I was off for a walk down the Main,
Where a late-night parade tramped the grungy terrain:
Ladies in tight shorts and men wearing skirts,
Eating "all-dressed steamies, with poutine for dessert.

Then all of a sudden there arose such a clatter
Even cops looked up to see what was the matter.
And what with my wondering eyes did I view,
But a tiny caleche pulled by 8 huge skidoos.

At the wheel was a plump man, all decked out in black
Sporting day-glo green sneakers and a pigtail in back.
One glance at him left me pale and shivering,
For behind his red beard, peeked a razor blade earring.

His moustache was twirled, his lips held a sneer,
He looked like a cross 'twixt King Kong and King Lear.
And all of a sudden it was clear as a bell,
I knew in a moment, t'was Santa from Hell.

He sprang from his carriage and gave me a glare,
Then frisked me for spare change, my arms in the air.
Then he took a long swig from a bottle of beer,
And gave me my gifts for the coming New Year.

Strikes by the Metro, post office, police,
A hole in The Roof, to cause us new grief,
A black magic marker along with guidelines,
For crossing apostrophes off all English signs.

Then he tossed in the GST tax, and Free Trade,
And emptied my wallet for the coming decade.
Then he grinned with a smile that spread ear to ear,
"Merry Christmas," he said. "I'll see you next year."

He leapt on his skidoo and revved it again,
And promised us this winter would never end.
"On January! On February! April and March!"
"Let Spring be icy and summer be harsh!

"You'll be skiing in June, shovelling snow in July,
"And battling a new bug — the *winter black fly*."
Then he stepped on the gas and sped out of sight,
In a cloud of pollution that blacked out the night.

I awoke in a tizzy and leapt from my bed,
And peered out my window, trembling with dread.
No skidoo. No Santa. Nothing was there.
Just the cold winter sweat of a Montreal nightmare.

Alien Life

SHOP 'N' SMUGGLE

•

•

•

It's a sunny summer weekend and you're looking for an active sport — something that requires the stamina of biking, the stealth of hunting and the nerve of rock-climbing. It's obviously time to head south to the U.S. for a quintessential Canadian weekend of Shop 'n' Smuggle.

The trip begins early Saturday morning when you unpack everything in the car to make room for your loot. You travel light — nothing but American dollars. The excitement begins an hour later when you pull into the U.S. border crossing, where a customs official examines you with x-ray eyes.

GUARD: Purpose of your visit?
YOU: Oh . . . a little sun, swimming and biking.
GUARD: Where are the bicycles?
YOU: Uh . . . we're gonna rent them.

Why tell him you plan to buy them in the States?

Minutes later you are in America, racing off an exit ramp for your first purchase. You've deliberately let your gas tank drop to empty. Now you fill it with U.S. gas till it drips on the pavement, feeling smug: You've already saved more money than you earn in a day.

Smuggling used to mean a dull day someplace like Forest Hills Factory Outlet — a vast, dreary warehouse in Winooski, Vermont that looked like a Consumers Distributing outlet in Moscow.

But with the rise of the Canadian dollar, the U.S has created new attractions to lure visiting Quebec smugglers — ENTIRE TOWNS that are factory outlets. These idyllic villages are nestled in the mountains of New England or New York State and exist for no reason whatsoever but to help Canadians shop.

You know you are approaching one by a sudden profusion of maple leaf flags, and signs saying things like: "We accept Canadian Tire money."

In fact no one seems to shop at factory outlet towns except us. Politically, we may be anti-American, but when it comes to buying consumer goods, there's no place like the U.S. of A.

At first glance, a factory outlet town looks like a Soviet teenager's

American fantasy — a place where the streets are paved with Levis. Entire blocks are filled with brand-name stores jammed cheek to jowl — Ralph Lauren, Timberland shoes, Nikes, Reeboks, Dansk and Calvin Klein — all sporting "SALE" signs.

Apparently no people live in these towns. The only other buildings are 24-hour banking machines.

Surrounding the towns are majestic mountains, lush forests, warm lakes — but who cares? Everyone is inside the outlets, rummaging madly through bins of clothing as if they've never seen a store.

Designer jeans and polo shirts fly through the air, fistfights break out over Calvin Klein blazers. It is a clothing version of a food riot.

Men search for manufacturing defects called "seconds": jackets with holes, shirts with no buttons, pants with no zippers and zippers with no pants. Women are more selective, concentrating on quality stuff: cashmere sweaters with tags that say things like:

"Suggested price: $2500. Our price: only $99."

After seven hours of racing from outlet to outlet, your family looks like it has run a marathon. You check into a motel, exhausted — but the challenge has just begun. Sure you've got the goods — but now you've got to get them into Canada.

You spend all night clipping telltale sales tags off your purchases, many sewed on with steel cable. You work feverishly. Your motel room looks like a textile sweatshop employing underage kids. You also make sure your new clothing looks old. You rub mud on your white sneakers, soak your jeans in the tub, and camp out on the hotel room floor all night, to give your new sleeping bags and tent an authentic odour. Next morning you burn your clothing receipts in the motel sink and prepare for re-entry into Canada. The clothes you wore are dumped in the hotel trash; you swaddle yourselves in new apparel — ignoring your kids' protests.

CHILD: Mom, why do I have to wear four pairs of underwear?
MOTHER: It's going to be cold . . . And remember, if the policemen at the border asks you anything, shuddup and let your father talk.

An hour later, you top up your gas tank and approach the Canadian border. Sales receipts fly by your window like snow, jettisoned by the long row of Canadian cars ahead of you. Some have pulled over to the side of the road where poorly organized families are busily changing clothes.

You discuss your border strategy with your spouse. You will say you've been gone since Friday, to allow the necessary 48 hours out of the country — in case you have to declare anything. But you'd rather not. You rehearse your lines:

138

BORDER GUARD: Have you purchased anything in the U.S.?
FAMILY: *(in unison)* NOTHING AT ALL.

At the border, there is a 45-minute lineup. As you inch up in line, your confidence wanes. A man has been caught with a price tag on his windsurfer. A family of four has been forced to remove the tarp atop their roof, revealing a piano. Another is caught trying to smuggle in a car.

You get nervous. Will the border guard be suspicious of your three wool sweaters? The four new bicycles? Maybe you shouldn't have bought the toboggan? — it *is* July.

You feel guilty, suddenly transformed from a law-abiding citizen into a criminal filled with secret shame. Like Raskolnikov in Crime and Punishment, you have a powerful compulsion to confess.

"I'm sorry, sir, I'm sorry . . . I thought the duty-free limit was $3000 — not $300."

The car ahead of you moves through. Suddenly it is your turn. A Canadian customs official leans into your window with a disarming smile.

OFFICIAL: When did you leave Canada?
HUSBAND: Friday morning.
WIFE: Friday night.
KID: No mom, it was Saturday morning!
OFFICIAL: Have you purchased any goods in the United States?
HUSBAND: Nope.
WIFE: Nothing at all.
CHILD: 24 pairs of underwear nine shirts, a new computer game . . .

The customs officer peers grimly into the back of the car, at the shiny new luggage set overflowing with enough shirts to clothe all of Mali; at the 15 pairs of sneakers, the piles of skirts and pants, the 30 boxes of Freihoffer's chocolate chip cookies from the Grand Union store.

He looks at your son: an onion-shaped ball padded in so many layers of clothing he has difficulty breathing; at your wife in her sneakers and black cocktail gown, and you in a bathing suit and $300 dress shoes.

He stares at you with a look that could penetrate steel, let alone your guilt-crazed eyes. He *knows*.

Just as you are about to confess everything and throw yourself on his mercy, he smiles and gives what looks like a wink.

"Have a good trip," he says, and waves you through the border and on your way home. He understands. He knows that you are just a small potato, a typical Canadian out for a weekend of Shop 'n' Smuggle.

That's how he plans to spend next weekend in Vermont.

HAVE AN ICE DAY

•

•

•

The waitress wore a "Hi! I'm Kim" button, and a smile that stretched from Florida to Arkansas.

"How are *you* this morning?" she asked, pouring a watery cup of coffee. Then she looked at me meaningfully and gushed: "HAVE A NICE MORNING."

It was the first day of my vacation, and there was little doubt I had crossed the border into the "States" — where every day is a nice day, regardless of the weather. In a ten-day jaunt across the eastern U.S. I shook hands with a dozen grocers, exchanged names with 50 waitresses, and was wished enough nice days to last me a lifetime.

My egg salad sandwiches came wrapped in paper announcing HAVE A HAPPY DAY. My restaurant bill was signed HAVE A WONDERFUL EVENING. I was given a ticket by a policeman who told me to HAVE A GOOD NIGHT. By the time I arrived home, I had met so many friendly Americans that my mouth hurt from smiling and my handshake had gone limp.

I was thankful to be back in sullen Canada.

A Canadian tourist in the U.S. notices many differences from home. There are better roads, bigger portions of food and more obese people. There are more national flags on any one block than in half of Canada. But nothing is more unnerving to many of us than the façade of cheerfulness that starts abruptly at the 49th parallel.

America may have crime on its streets, shoot-outs on its expressways, and syringes littering its beaches — but there is a smile on every face and a chirpy greeting in every pocket. And the worst of it is that visitors are expected to participate — from the first "Howdy" to the final handshake.

A typical American restaurant experience goes something like this:

WAITRESS: *(smiling)* HI! How're you folks this evening?
ME: OK . . . Hungry, actually.
WAITRESS: GREAT . . . My name is Sue and I'll be your serving person for this evening . . . Where are *you* folks from?
ME: *(reluctantly)* Uh . . . Montreal, actually.
WAITRESS: Mawn-treal! Oh, that's such a *neat* city. I always wanted to visit there . . . I guess you folks are French, huh?

ME: Uh, no actually. Could we ord–

WAITRESS: I once took French in school, but I don't really remember it . . . Bawn-jour. Ha ha! Parlez-vous. Ha ha!

ME: Ha ha! . . . Uh . . . . We're kind of in a hurry. Would it be possible to order?"

WAITRESS: Oh, SURE! What'll you folks be having to drink? The beverage of the evening is a Banana-Mash-with-peach-liqueur-riple-sec-and-fresh-cream-and-strawberries.

ME: Uhhh, no . . . just food, please.

WAITRESS: Sure, that's GREAT . . . But I only serve drinks. The other serving person will take your food order . . . She'll be by real soon. HAVE A GREAT EVENING.

When the "other serving person" finally arrives fifteen minutes later the same procedure is repeated, as it is for the busperson, the dessert person and all the other persons who want to get to know me.

Throughout the meal they will buzz around my table like mosquitoes asking: "How's your meal?" "Everything OK?" at every bite. Each time they ask I feel compelled to answer, although I know they do not want to hear the truth.

If I were to say: "The green beans taste like paper clips and the spaghetti like it was boiled in the box," my waitress would look terribly hurt.

"I know," she would say, red-faced. "The regular cook is on his night off, so there's not much I can do . . . But try the Chocolate A-bomb for dessert. It's *real* good."

Moments after she left, another smiling serving person would be by and chirp: "HI! . . . how's your meal tonight?"

Some Montreal friends of mine have spent the last ten summers in Cape Cod, and it's gradually worn them out.

"When I go to a restaurant, I don't want to have a relationship with my waitress," says one. All this smiling and saying "Fine. Great . . . Delicious!" is driving me crazy. I'd rather eat at home . . . It's less work."

What is the source of America's good cheer, and why don't Canadians share it? Are they just friendly, while we are a nation of grouches? Or is there more?

Some blame the difference on the weather. In the U.S. people can wish you a nice day, because most of the time it's at least superficially true.

In Canada, good days are rare — and what would we say the rest of the year?

"Have a damp and frost-bitten day?"

Others blame our differences on history. The U.S. is a melting pot where every citizen is the same, a fellow American, you are expected to pretend to love.

Canada, on the other hand, is a nation of minorities: a community of uncommunicative communities. We have learned to tolerate our differences — even celebrate them — but there is no pretence that we must love each other.

Your waitress lets you eat your meal in peace, and you do the same for her. That's confederation.

In truth, America's "Have a nice day" syndrome is an irreconcilable difference between us and them. It is an intrusion into our solitude, an affront to our timidity, an assault on our well-earned gloom. We must stand on guard against it.

My Cape Cod friends recently tested a new defense. The last time they went to a U.S. restaurant they brought along a dozen friends. When the waitress flashed her opening smile, they beat her to the punch.

"HI . . . I'm Jerry," said one of them smiling back. "I'm from Montreal — I'm a lawyer. This is Lucy. She's from Montreal too — she's in film. That's Larry . . ."

Before he was halfway around the table the waitress turned tail and fled for the kitchen; she didn't say another word all night — in fear of provoking a new round of introductions.

So the next time you visit the U.S., try taking your whole hotel out for dinner and see what happens. It may be the most intimate dinner you have all vacation.

In the meantime, HAVE AN ICE DAY.

CLOSE ENCOUNTER
AT 35,000 FEET

.

.

.

When I boarded the plane in Miami, she was sitting in my seat — a stocky woman of about 70 with the body of a bulldog and a will to match.

"It's OK," she announced in a thick Eastern-European accent. "You sit there by window. I am here first."

She smiled, sweetly. "Be a good boy, eh . . . I'm an old lady."

I said that I'd reserved an aisle seat a week earlier because I disliked flying and got dizzy at the window. She argued some more — but I insisted.

"You'll be sorry," she grumbled, reluctantly yielding the seat. "I go to the bathroom every ten minutes and you'll have to move."

Beneath my seat (and hers) there was no room for my bag because she'd filled it with huge sacks of oranges and grapefruit. I opened the overhead bin, more oranges and grapefruit tumbled out.

"They're not mine," she lied smoothly. "You should have come earlier. You came too late."

Resigned, I sat down, holding my bag in my lap; instantly she started to talk — an endless monologue that accompanied me all the way home.

"We were supposed to leave ten minutes earlier . . . we're going to be late. *Mine God!* There are so many people here . . . it gives me a headache this travel.

"And money! It costs so much for a hotel in Miami it's not worth it. $400 for the flight and $1500 for the hotel — just for five little weeks in the sun.

"How can they charge so much for a hotel, tell me? " she sighed. "Thanks God at least I can go."

When we hit cruising altitude, she thrust me her duty-free form and a pen. "Please mister, I don't understand nothing . . . you can write?"

I asked her what she had to declare.

"Nothing," she replied matter-of factly, oblivious to the truckload of oranges at her feet. "You're such a nice boy. I'm so lucky you sat beside me."

"Tell me, you have a car? . . . Maybe you can give me a lift home when we get to Montreal?"

Mercifully, there was a movie on board which I settled in to watch. But

143

she was hard of hearing, and asked me to repeat every second line. Minutes felt like hours, and I pretended to sleep. When the flight attendants came by, my seatmate ordered an orange juice and two tomato juices she quickly stockpiled under my seat; I ordered a small bottle of wine and in seconds she was eyeing it covetously.

"You paid a lot for that?"

"No," I said "It's free."

"Free?" Why don't they say so? . . . Hmmm, maybe I should have one too."

She turned and shouted at the steward.

"Mister! . . . Two bottles of wine!"

"In a moment, madam," he replied politely, and continued serving another passenger.

"Mister!" she hollered a second time.

The steward glared at her, hissing: "I have other passengers too, madam."

"Okay okay, I'm only asking," she said. "I thought maybe you didn't hear and I'm very thirsty. I'm just an old lady and I . . ."

Resigned, the steward trudged over and handed her two small bottles of wine. The moment he turned his back, she slipped them into her purse and whispered:

"Such a nice gift for my neighbours. You know, I never drink."

The flight dragged on and so did her performance, as she battled with flight attendants and fellow passengers alike. Other travellers glared at me, assuming I was her son and should somehow control her outbursts. True to her word she went to the bathroom a dozen times, crawling over me in her battered Adidas sneakers. She was built like a battleship and weighed almost as much.

Yet somehow, between the bathroom breaks and the battles, her life story came out in snatches. She was a survivor of the Holocaust, a number still tattooed on her arm as a horrible reminder.

"My whole family was killed by Hitler," she said — every brother, every cousin, everybody but her.

Somehow she had escaped to the woods where she'd lived alone for two years, shunning human contact, eating anything to survive, until the war finally ended and she fled to Canada.

"It's easy today for a nice young man like you in a nice happy world — but I had to push my way through this life, fighting every inch for what I got.

"Believe me, in this world no one looks after you except you. And it doesn't matter what anyone else thinks."

By the time we began our descent into Montreal, I had come to understand — perhaps even like — her. And I think she liked me.

"I'm so lucky God sent you," she trilled. "You're such a good boy . . . You should only be my grandson."

I was relieved that I wasn't, but pleased by the compliment; it showed that with a little understanding you could get along with almost anyone.

"PREPARE FOR THE FINAL DESCENT," announced the flight attendant and I settled back in my chair and braced for the landing. The plane burst through the final clouds and hurtled toward earth.

Suddenly, my companion unbuckled her seatbelt and leapt to her feet, trying to climb over me toward the overhead luggage rack. The plane was in full descent, bouncing turbulently, and even the flight attendants were securely buckled in.

"Hold it!" I shouted, pushing her back into her seat protectively. "You can't do this on a plane. It's dangerous . . . just wait another minute."

"Let me up!" she barked. "I have to beat the others or I'll be stuck in the plane. Please move!"

I held her a moment more, concerned about her safety, but she erupted in rage.

"*You're not my mother!*" she screamed. "I don't need a mother and I didn't ask for one. *Out of my way!*"

She leapt to her feet again just as the plane landed with a thump, and she fell sprawling onto my lap. She pushed herself up again and scrambled atop my seat — and me — triumphantly wrenching open the luggage rack.

The plane was now speeding down the runway but every flight attendant on board was up and rushing toward us, shouting:

"Sit down madam! Sit down!"

It was like trying to stop a cannonball. She stood on the seat, rummaging through the luggage bin, even while they shouted at her, until finally the plane slowed to a near-stop. She grabbed her sacks of oranges and grapefruit and stormed down the aisle before anyone else was even out of their seat. But first she turned and glared at me, and announced for the whole plane to hear:

"I'm sorry I ever asked you for help. I don't need *anyone's* help!"

Exhausted, I lay back in my seat and waited for the plane to empty. I wanted to avoid the other passengers and hoped to put as much distance as possible between my seatmate and myself. In fact, it was only after 40 minutes and two drinks at the airport bar that I finally ventured downstairs to pick up my luggage and get a cab.

As I stepped outside the terminal, the taxi attendant was shouting, "I'm not giving you another cab! I've given you six already and you're not getting a seventh."

I backed quickly out of sight as I heard a familiar booming voice:

"Mine God! They want $25 to take me home — it's so expensive! I'm just an old lady. Why won't somebody give me a ride?"

As she spoke a young couple pushed by her and leapt into a cab, slamming the door before she could scramble in behind them.

The wind was blowing. Snow was falling in torrents. She stood forlornly on the pavement, surrounded by her luggage and her huge sacks of fruit. Resigned to my fate, I stepped into view, and her face lit up like I was her oldest friend.

"Mister! Mister! Thanks God you're still here! Maybe you'd like to share a taxi?"

ALL QUIET ON THE
NORTHERN FRONT

.

.

.

In the American film *True Believer*, actor James Woods, playing a lawyer, asks his assistant to track down two witnesses. She tells him that one is dead, and the other has moved to Canada.

"Same thing," Woods says laconically, then tells her to forget it.

Only days after seeing the film, I was reading Britain's *Manchester Guardian* and noticed a story about Wellington, the capital city of New Zealand. It was described as: "A place so boring even the Canadians seem interesting."

Neither remark was really unusual. They were just routine spears flung into the tattered hide of the Canadian, a maligned, insulted and allegedly dull creature said to be only slightly more exciting than the mollusk.

An Ottawa columnist reports being told that "one Canadian is as boring as three Swiss or five Belgians."

A British survey asks people what comes to mind when they hear the word "Canada." The answer: "rocks."

The respected *Economist* magazine pronounces us "more boring than all other nations, except Singapore."

What is going on? Am I just sensitive or are we really a nation of limp flapjacks — the polyester of the international set. Whither this image of the dull Canadian?

Personally I think it's a bum rap — the result of living next to the most opinionated, loud-mouthed nation on earth. I noticed the difference again recently on a trip to Costa Rica, where most tourists are from the U.S. or Canada. The two groups look identical, but you can locate the Americans the moment you walk into a room — by their sound.

"The skiing in my state is absolutely *unreal*," a young American will be saying, as if through a megaphone. "I mean we are talking *mega*-skiing here, totally merciless . . . AWESOME."

He is describing an obscure hill in Idaho, barely larger than Montreal's Mount Royal. Yet ask the Canadians at the next table about skiing the Rockies and they'll reply:

"Well, it depends on the season. It can be quite impressive in winter — if it's not too crowded, or too foggy, or too wet."

Canadians are a nation of qualifiers, ever cautious, obsessed with accuracy and truth. Our national image pays heavily for this trait, especially when compared to our larger-than-life neighbours. Unlike us, Americans talk to entertain, with little concern for truth. Chicago is "the greatest town on earth." The Philadelphia Flyers are the "world champions." Their corner restaurant makes "the best French food you'll ever taste."

Who can possibly keep up? As a journalist I'm aware of the difference between us every time I cross the border to cover a story.

Whether I interview a U.S. senator or a gas station attendant, Americans reply in colourful "clips" — punchy made-for-television anecdotes fired out in machine gun-like bursts.

Not us. Put a Yankee and a Canuck at a hotel fire, and they describe different events.

REPORTER: What happened?

AMERICAN: It was awesome. I heard a rumble, then KAPOW!! — there was this incredible explosion — flames everywhere! It was like hell, only worse.

CANADIAN: I heard the sound of the explosion . . . well actually, I didn't know it was an explosion at the time. It was more like . . . a . . . *thumping* sound.

REPORTER: *(eager for dramatic clip for news)* What then?

CANADIAN: Well, I put on my bathrobe to investigate . . . I went downstairs, and there was . . . well I couldn't actually *see* the fire . . . but I certainly saw a good deal of smoke.

REPORTER: *(desperate)* How did you *feel?* Weren't you scared?

CANADIAN: Ah . . . it's not really fair for me to answer. I wasn't in the best place to see the fire . . . My wife had a better angle, didn't you dear?

WIFE: *(in bathrobe, popping awake)* Oh no, not really dear. You were in a better position than me . . . Really, I was looking after Nathan.

CANADIAN: No, no dear . . . I'm almost sure you were closer than I wa—

(Reporter rushes off to find more Americans staying at hotel)

After several years of cross-continent reporting I've come to the conclusion that finding clips, like growing grapes, has a lot to do with the sun. The further north you go the leaner the harvest. Take the American south. People there talk in a slow drawl, but invariably deliver pearls, like:

"Son, your reasoning is about as bumpy as a moose's rump."

Hit New York and it's all hype. People's hands wave about like a conductor's and superlatives are the only form of adjective.

149

Everything is "stupendous . . . unique . . . divine."

As you approach the border, good clip fades as fast as sunshine. Even in northern Maine you can already hear the earnest Canadian tones of an Edmund Muskie; by the time you reach Montreal or Toronto, lively clips must be extracted like molars, unwilling to leave the mouth.

The hands have stopped moving. Hyperbole has vanished. Adjectives are scarce — replaced by qualifiers like "somewhat" and "possibly."

This linguistic modesty is most visible in the heart of Canada — the far north — where people ration words like wood for a fire. Typical is a Whitehorse musher I interviewed during a dogsled race several years ago. He was about to leave for three weeks alone in the bush and I tried vainly to get a dramatic quote out of him.

— Are you worried about the weather? I asked.
— Nope.
— But storms can be dangerous when you're alone? You could die.
— Yep.
— What about your dogs? Isn't it tough on them?
— I haven't asked 'em.

This northern silence may have meaning. On one icy journey in the north, I pestered my Inuit guide David with a litany of questions: Why did he seem so comfortable in the cold? How come his fingers didn't freeze when he took his gloves off to work? Why wasn't he shivering — like me?

After a series of patient, laconic replies, he offered some unexpected advice: "Words take energy, Josh . . . They burn up heat. If you talk less, you'll be more warm."

It was the last thing he said to me for hours. Reluctantly, I was forced to take his advice, and the quieter I became, the warmer I got.

Perhaps it is from here — this Darwinian need for silence — that Canadians have evolved. And developed our undeserved reputation as dull.

Wrapped in thick parkas, toques pulled over our ears, brains busily thinking about how to start the car, we are less generous of breath, less quick to expound than our Southern neighbours.

It's not that we're boring. We've just got better things to do than talk about the weather. Like survive it.

TERMINAL FRUSTRATION

•

•

•

MIAMI AIRPORT. 1:00 P.M. : I have stopped here on my way back from Mexico, and entered airport hell. It's the end of Christmas holidays and every Canadian in Florida is lined up at the Air Canada desk — tanned, rested and ready to kill to get on a plane before me.

At one wicket, a man from Quebec has been battling for 15 minutes. Only three of his seats are together; his travel agent promised him five. At another wicket, a huge Toronto woman is demanding a vegetarian meal — she can't "digest" beef — and a sunburned man holds an elasticized dog leash attached to a remarkably fat poodle he claims is "carry-on luggage."

"She only weighs 10 pounds — at most 11," he tells the ticket agent. "She'll sit on my lap."

Overwhelmed by luggage, Air-Canada's conveyer belt has seized up. Enormous piles of baggage grow like slag heaps at every counter sprouting tennis rackets, skateboards and surfboards.

Porters shout, kids in Disneyland hats wail, exhausted ticket agents bark. Crowds push against me like food rioters. Beside me a refined-looking woman sighs: "Sometimes I don't understand people . . . They get to an airport and turn into wild animals."

I nod smugly. Why rush? My flight doesn't leave till 2:10 p.m.

1:15 P.M. : The ticket counter is still tied up. The Quebec fellow has four seats together — but still demands five; the man with the poodle is told his dog weighs 27 pounds — but he still wants her on board. A heavy set man I dimly remember from high school pushes through the crowd and drops his bag in front of the poodle. The poodle's owner removes the bag and places it behind the dog.

"Hey! That's *my* bag," roars my former classmate. "No one touches my bag without asking. *No one.*"

"*My* dog was there first!" retorts the Poodle man.

"Oh yeah!" bellows my classmate, replacing his suitcase. "You touch my bag again — you're dog meat!"

The baggage conveyer lurches to life. Porters start flinging luggage onto it like garbage bags; one grabs my suitcase and tosses it on before it's been tagged: Lord knows what country it's off to! I shout desperately at a ticket agent and she lunges for the suitcase seconds before it disappears down the chute.

"You must be from Canada," she barks. "In Miami, you never let go of *anything.*"

1:30 P.M. : The Quebec man yields the counter and the Refined woman steps forward. A woman lunges out of nowhere in near hysteria.

"*Please!*" she says in a thick Parisian accent. "My husband . . . he just arrive in zee ambulance! He is very sick. I must get him on zee plane."

The Refined woman's gentle features harden like quick-dry cement. "I-have-been-standing-here-for-one-hour," she hisses.

"*I-am-next.*"

"Mais, mon mari — my husband — zee ambulance!"

"He can *wait* his turn like everyone else!"

The two women snap at each other, joining the battleground. Am I the only sane person left?

1:42 P.M. : The Refined woman marches off, triumphantly gripping her boarding pass. At last, it's my turn — but the Paris woman cuts in front of me.

"*Please,*" she begs. "My husband . . . zee ambulance!"

"Yes ma'am," says the ticket agent, ignoring me. "We'll take you now."

Tears streak down the Paris woman's cheeks. What can I say?

1:55 P.M. : The Paris woman is making plans complex enough for an intergalactic voyage. Her flight leaves in an hour, mine in 15 minutes.

FINAL CALL FOR MONTREAL. ALL PASSENGERS SHOULD NOW BE ON BOARD.

My classmate and Mr. Poodle are long gone. I address the ticket agent: "I'm trying to be reasonable — but will I catch the Montreal plane?"

"Montreal?" she snaps. "I can't promise that sir. You should already be on board. You'll have to wait your turn and see."

What to do? I'm lost in the jungle, doomed to turn into a savage. Should I shout, scream, hiss? Emulate my highschool mate and threaten to turn everyone into dogmeat?

FINAL CALL FOR MONTREAL.

I feel the kindly Dr. Josh turning into vile Mr. Hyde. Frustration, rage and guilt churn together. Blood rises to my head and reason vanishes. I am seconds from exploding . . .

The ticket agent looks up casually at the Parisian lady: "You know, this gentleman's flight leaves in a few minutes. Perhaps I should deal with him first even if he was late."

2:03 P.M. : I am rushing down "Corridor G" like an escaped criminal, a sweaty hand on my luggage, I get through U.S. customs. Five minutes to go. Through the metal detector. Two minutes to go. Down a long, long hallway, shouting "Gangway! Gangway!" — into the boarding area.

It's totally deserted but my plane is still there. I scramble aboard and fall into my seat exhausted, drenched — ready for another vacation.

The plane doesn't leave for 45 minutes.

CURTAIN CALL IN CUBA

•

•

•

There are some stories I'd rather not be in Montreal when I tell. Since I'm leaving on vacation, I thought I'd share one with you: the Adventure of the Gringo in the Bath Curtain, the most embarrassing experience of my life.

It took place on a visit to Cuba, in the late 1960s. The country had just opened up to tourism and Cubans were fascinated by foreigners: curious about what we wore, what we earned, what we thought.

A handful of resorts had been built but they were still in the embryonic stages, virtual compounds where guests ate at large communal tables, and every meal was the same — fish — for dinner, lunch and breakfast.

I shared a small cell-like room with a Quebecer named Alain. There was one small luxury: We each had our own private bathroom — out in the hall.

Things went smoothly until the third day of my stay. That night, Alain went off to shower in his bathroom, and I toddled off to mine. I stepped out into the corridor and felt a sudden gust of wind from the balcony. To my horror, the door to our room slammed shut, locking me out — stark naked.

Alain stepped out of his bathroom; he was undressed too. It was insane. Two pale-white, naked gringos stranded in a hotel corridor in Castro's Cuba. What the hell were we going to do?

The door to our room was as solid as communism's grip on the country. There were no towels in the bathroom to cover ourselves. Not even a washcloth.

Alain fled to the washroom and refused to come out, mortified at the prospect of being caught nude, determined to sleep in the bathtub. I had another idea.

The one removable object in my washroom was a shower curtain: a heavy industrial sheet of plastic with pink flamingos on it. I ripped it off the rod, wrapped it round my waist and tied it in a knot — a Polynesian-style skirt made of Saran Wrap. I had never felt more ridiculous in my life . . . .

Furtively, I slipped down to the lobby looking for a hotel employee to help me. It was only 11:00 p.m. but the reception area was deserted: The staff had abandoned us for the night. I would have to go outside.

My hotel was situated on the main drag of town. It was Friday night and a lively fiesta was taking place at a nearby park. The street was filled with people, swaying to the sound of salsa music.

I stepped outside, trying to look nonchalant in my bathtub toga; I might as well have been dressed as a U.S. Marine. In seconds every person in three blocks had turned to stare. Many Cubans had never seen a foreigner before — let alone a half-naked one, dressed in a shower curtain.

My room was right over the street, on the second floor — some 10 feet over my head. The balcony door was open, and I looked up in despair. How was I going to get in?

As I spoke no Spanish, I approached a group of men and tried to play charades. I pointed at my room. I twisted my hand as if I was turning a key. I pounded on an imaginary door. They looked at me as if I was crazy.

A crowd was growing, pointing at me, whispering, laughing. I rushed back into the hotel lobby and emerged with a rickety old chair. I placed it under my balcony and pointed at my room again: Could no one understand my predicament?

Two young men cautiously approached, gaping at the flamingos on my shower curtain. But they seemed to understand . . .

They gripped the chair firmly and I stepped up on it, then climbed slowly up onto the narrow chair back. I still couldn't reach the balcony — so the men grabbed my bare legs and hoisted me in the air.

My outstretched fingers grasped the edge of the balcony floor and I tried to chin myself up. I kicked my legs desperately and lunged my hand at the balcony railing — and the unthinkable happened:

The shower curtain slipped from my body and fell to the ground. I hung in mid-air like a plucked chicken, completely naked. I was so embarrassed I thought I would die.

Behind me, I heard a loud cheer. More Cubans had obviously arrived and they began to clap rhythmically. I heard the word "gringo, gringo," shouted again and again. Half the town seemed to be there.

Dismally, I chinned myself up the balcony railing, inch by inch, sweating in the tropical heat, as the crowd cheered and hooted words in Spanish. Finally, I got one knee onto the ledge, then the other.

I climbed over the railing onto my balcony and turned to look. Several hundred Cubans were now watching — teenagers, grandmothers, children — all roaring with laughter. They had abandoned the fiesta for a better show: me.

What could I do? Standing naked atop my small stage, I tipped an imaginary hat and bowed; then I turned on my heels and fled into my room. Behind me the applause went on and on, the largest ovation I have ever received — and probably ever will.

The next morning, I slipped into the dining room for the communal fish breakfast, hoping none of my fellow tourists had heard what happened. As I entered, they rose and applauded, loud and long. My late-night antics had awakened the whole hotel, and many guests had enjoyed the show from their bedroom windows.

For the rest of my stay I was an unwitting celebrity. Cubans gathered regularly on the street outside my window, hoping for a repeat performance of "el gringo en la cortina del baño" — the gringo in the shower curtain — a story that had become legend overnight.

Undoubtedly it is still told in the bars and cantinas of the town today, though I have never gone back to find out. And wherever I travel, I always wear my shorts in the shower.

CANADIAN AUTOMOBILE
TRILOGY : 3

.

.

.

Josh Freed
Montreal,
June 9, 1990.

Dear Vandal:

At last, I am getting to know you, though not as well as you know me.

Last week, I wrote to you, complaining you had stolen my car — after several years of removing it piece by piece.

When I wrote you, the car had been missing for a week. But two days later I got a call from police saying you had returned it. You'd dropped my car off in northeast Montreal, in front of a bus stop. The door had been forced open, the steering-wheel lock was snapped, and you'd hot-wired the ignition.

The car sported several new dents and scratches and wouldn't start. It was towed to a garage where it's been ever since.

Worse than the physical damage you inflicted was the psychological, for you violated my car. You went through every intimate corner as thoroughly as a tax auditor, perusing each shred of paper, taking what you wanted and leaving me the debris.

By now, you know a lot about me — but I know something about you too. Clues to your identity were everywhere, in what you took and in what you left behind.

First, the driver's seat was so close to the dashboard that a 10-year-old could barely squeeze in. Obviously, you are exceptionally short; you may even be a child vandal.

Your girlfriend is the same size. I assume she's a girl because she left the make-up mirror flipped down on the passenger side — along with some Coke stains on the seat.

Judging by your garbage you had a wild week. There were empty

Budweiser bottles, a Dunkin Donuts box, hot dog wrappers, french fry containers and a diet Pepsi cup that had obviously been full of ice. (Given your diet, I thought you might be an off-duty policeman).

Then there was the radio. I was glad to see it was still there, but puzzled that it was tuned to CBC FM. It was difficult to imagine you on a week-long joyride — guzzling beer, chomping on jellydonuts and rocking to the sound of Rachmaninoff's Suite for Piano, Opus 3.

I was also surprised by your neatness. Despite your garbage, the car was considerably cleaner than when you took it — partly because you'd cleaned out everything of value. My car is generally so messy people sometimes ask me if it's been robbed — but you managed to make it look respectable.

You sifted through the trunk, the glove compartment, every nook and cranny, taking pennies, pencils and penknives. You removed old sweatshirts, old newspapers and old carparts. I think you may even have vacuumed.

There were no butts in the ashtray; in fact, you threw out some that had been there for months. Obviously you are a fervent anti-smoker.

You also like the outdoors. That's why you stole my camping gear, isn't it? You took two sleeping bags, some air mattresses, a giant flashlight and a tent — though you left the mosquito net and the tentfly behind.

I guess you like to rough it.

And you like to take car trips, especially in other peoples cars. You put 800 kilometres on my odometer.

I was glad to see you like exercise. You took my tennis racket, a football and an old pair of size 10 basketball shoes. But you passed up an excellent assortment of cross-country ski wax. Perhaps you prefer downhill.

Your intellectual life disappointed me. I'd harboured fantasies you were a political thief, stealing because you think property is theft. Yet your choice of reading material leaves much to be desired. You passed up *Traitor To My Heart*, a South African book that's received rave reviews, as well as a hardcover biography of Louis Riel, and a copy of *Trotsky: My Life*, wedged under the spare tire.

Not that you don't have a literary side. You grabbed an issue of *Sports Illustrated*, and *Killshot*, a best-selling detective thriller by Elmore Leonard.

Finally, you took an expensive manual on the art of screen-writing that's practically impossible to replace. This intrigues me.

Perhaps you are an aspiring scriptwriter. An ex-con, hoping to sell your story as a movie (*Hot-Wiring Cars: My Life*). A teenager with an idea for another violent flick: *Revenge of the Vandal*. If my manual comes in handy, I think I deserve a screen credit?

Over-all, what do I make of the evidence? Hot dog wrappers, donut boxes and classical music. Camping equipment, an empty astray and another broken mirror. A suspect who is tiny with short legs, but arms powerful enough to snap the steering wheel lock.

Like Colombo, I pore over the clues, reassembling them again and again in different order, obsessed with who you are. Could you be a midget wrestler who dreams of writing movies? An off-duty policeman with a taste for Debussy and donuts?

An anti-smoking zealot camped out on Mount Royal, vandalizing cars as part of your war on pollution.

I still require some details to complete my composite picture: one last clue that will allow me to identify the person in my driver's seat. I guess I'll have to wait for the next time you break into my car and go for a spin. And unfortunately, I suspect that won't be too long.

In the meantime, could you do me another favour? Please photocopy the screen-writing manual and mail it to me. And, let me know what you thought of the Elmore Leonard book.

If you like it, I can always leave another one on the drivers seat. You know how to get in.